Grandma Knows the F Word

Andy,
Live your dreams – Have Fun!
Ted

Ted Schredd knows fun.
The Edmonton Sun

Thank you for brightening our day.
Brian Adler - MTV

Grandma Knows the F Word is a kick in the pants!
Page Half Full Book Reviews

The book is 'F'enomenal! Ted Schredd is a regular guest on my radio program because he is an inspiration and a model for how to bring more feeling, friends and frivolity into life!
Buzz Bishop - Z95.3 FM Vancouver

It's about time someone told it like it is! This is a fabulous book, it really did change the way I look at people and things in my world.
Sarah Martin - Vancouver, BC

Ted Schredd has the insight, wisdom (and guts) to write about FUN in an inspiring and practical action-based way.
Jono Willcox - Pinnacle Pursuits Corporate Team Building

This book really flies in the face of the self help genre. Through cartoons and wise words, Ted provides a paint-by-numbers system to get some serious fun back into your life.
David Carlisle - Buxton, Derbyshire United Kingdom

I like your book. Easy on the eye and fun to read. I'll probably steal large segments of your book and put them in my book.
Steve Donahue - ***Author of Shifting Sands - A Guidebook for Crossing the Deserts of Change***

Grandma Knows the F Word

How adults can discover more fun in their lives

Written and Illustrated
by Ted Schredd

Discover Fun Publishing / Vancouver

Reprinted 2003, 2004
Discover Fun Publishing - Vancouver
PO Box 54082, Lonsdale West RPO, North Vancouver, BC V7M 3L5

Edited by Carolyn Bateman
Proofread by Elizabeth McLean
Cover design by Ted Schredd
Interior design by Ted Schredd
Photos by Ted Schredd, RJ Sauer, Nick Didlick, Roger Kintz, Melissa Smart and Richard Bender

Printed and bound in Canada by Transcontinental Printing

Canadian Cataloguing in Publication Data

Schredd, Ted

Grandma knows the F word : How adults can discover more fun intheir lives

ISBN 0-9731197-2-1

1. Conduct of life--Humor. I. Title.

BJ1595.S36 2002 158.1'02'07 C2002-903014-5

The publisher would like to acknowledge whoever made grilled cheese sandwich makers. Thank you, whoever you are.

This book is
dedicated to all
the people who
have inspired me
to enjoy life.

If you think you already
know how to have fun...
What reason could you
possibly give that would
justify not having more?

Contents

About the Author

By Kevin Thomson

My friendship with Ted began with a simple greeting that turned into a wild bicycle ejection. We met at a mountain bike race–he was racing and I was in the crowd. As he rounded the corner I cheered him on. During his negotiation of the corner, he lost control of the bike, flipped over his handlebars, and crashed into the fence. Without any trace of hostility, he rose from the dust and responded with "Woo-hoo!" He came over smiling and shook my hand, then got back on his bike and finished the race. We have been friends ever since.

Ted has often risen from the dust with a smile and a good attitude. When he cycled 8000 miles around North America he left his home in Vancouver, BC, with no money or camping gear, but relied on his sense of fun and adventure to guide him. No matter how many ditches he had to sleep in, he still kept going. His best-selling book, *The Cycling Adventures of Coconut Head*, is based on this amazing experience.

Ted has had a host of wacky jobs, such as skiing videographer in the Rocky Mountains, a frisbee instructor and cycling traffic reporter for a major market radio station. He has also worked as a host for a breakfast TV show, and most recently as a photographer who travels around the world taking pictures of destination resorts.

Ted enjoys himself most when he's near people who are experiencing fun. And if those people are not altogether familiar with fun, then he does whatever he can to get them involved. Ted can make fun, fun for anybody, even those who didn't think it was possible.

Spending time with Ted is like a day at the amusement park while receiving pleasure intravenously. He's a constant source of excitement and rushes, mingled with plenty of laughs and giggles. I have been fortunate to spend many quality moments watching his ideas grow into the monument of epiphanies that you now hold in your hand.

Through Ted you will see a new world where fun is not just a possibility, but rather an obvious companion in most situations. Some of these chapters will have you laughing; others will have you rethinking your life. But with Ted as your guide, you'll have a friend to inspire you to love your life. Have a great ride and watch out for the Mind Poo!

Introduction

It seems as if there is a self-help book on everything nowadays. Everything but how to have fun. There are books on love, happiness, business, divorce, dating, cooking, golf, fashion, nearly every activity and emotion there is; everything but fun. I could find books on where to have fun, what activities are fun and what time of the year to participate, but I was never able to find a book on how. Now, it would seem to me that a book on how to have fun would be a pretty important piece of literature for the world considering the state we're in. So yee-ha, here it is.

Every self-help book I have ever read is a little more entertaining than watching paint dry, but not much. Not to say that a serious style of self-help information presentation is a bad thing, it just never had me laughing while I improved my new-age self. So, as I wrote this book, my goal was to stimulate your funny bone and stimulate your mind. Hey, if it's going to be a book on fun, it may as well be fun too, right?

One of the people who taught me a lot about fun was Grandma Schredd. At ninety-four, Grandma still used a push lawnmower and grew most of her own food. She wasn't a really outgoing individual, but she seemed extremely content till her health began to turn at the age of ninety-six and eventually she passed away a couple of months before her 100th birthday. Grandma Schredd never complained and she was always thoughtful of others. She always had a smile and was quick to do what she felt like.

Grandma inspired me to get my mental act together so that I could have a happy fulfilling life regardless of what I did or didn't have. I learned from her that everybody has their own groove in life, and even though her idea of fun was extremely different from mine, it didn't mean that my method, her method or anybody else's techniques was the best way to have fun.

For the past fifteen years, I have been researching fun. That includes fun careers, lifestyle activities and ways of thinking. I have been studying and admiring fun people. Along the way I found tremendous inspiration from seniors. Like my Grandma's sister, who just turned ninety-eight at the time this was published. Last year she knitted more than 200 pairs of mittens for the Salvation Army. Then there is Betty Jean, who just ran a half marathon in under two hours at the age of seventy-four. Or sixty-nine-year-old Harvey who ran, cycled and paddled in a 100-kilometre adventure race. Then there was Clarence, who started downhill skiing at the age of sixty-five. Or Michael who went white water rafting for his eightieth birthday. And the list goes on and on.

I have met hundreds of down-to-earth and joyous people who always seemed to be genuinely happy with whatever they had. They all had a way of thinking that hopefully I have broken down and captured in words and drawings for you to comprehend: what they do, how they think and any other activity that might teach us how to have more fun in our lives. I think I have finally figured out a good portion of it and am proud to present it to you today.

All these people's skills and character traits have been molded into the symbol of Grandma Schredd. Like Santa Claus is to Christmas, Grandma Schredd is to fun. Everybody celebrates Christmas in their own way and so too with fun. So when I talk about Grandma Schredd, I am talking about what fun means to you personally. Grandma Schredd will offer advice and tips and pop into the book every once in a while to help guide the under-funned members of humanity to discover giggle enlightenment.

Having fun is more than having a good time at a party; it is a way of living. In order to get there you will have to get rid of some of the unpleasant things in your life. You will need to question yourself, your activities, your habits and your goals to help you clarify just why you are not living up fully to your fun potential. So the first part of the book is a little heavy. We will talk about anger, fear, sadness, guilt, jealousy and all those other icky little feelings. But don't worry, it gets better. If you make a commitment to more joy in your life, you will then learn about appreciation, children, silliness, spontaneity and more. We will talk about laughing, friends, judgment and competition. The last part of the book will help you to bring more fun into your home and your workplace.

Fun is for everybody–the president needs it, the queen needs it, emergency workers, office wworkers, doctors, lawyers, street people, everybody needs fun and more of it. If you are already having some, why not have some more? Fun has evolved considerably in the past fifty years or so. Not only is it OK and available, it has multiplied in possibility. There are more opportunities, more techniques, more difficult adrenaline sports and more societal acceptance than at any other time in history. But even though there is more access to fun, our lives have become more complicated. We are searching for ways to regain some fun in our lives.

Whether it is conscious, unconscious or habitual, we as individuals choose to have or not to have fun on a moment-by-moment basis. Having fun is truly up to you, so when you read through this book, look at it through your heart and not your head. Grandma Schredd and I personally invite you into the book and hopefully inspire you to go out and have more fun in life. Go for it and have fun.

Most of us have no problem having fun while on vacation. The challenge is, all the other days of the year. All you need to do is give yourself permission.

Ted Schredd

What is Fun?

The constitution only gives people the right to pursue happiness. You have to catch it yourself. Ben Franklin

There are more than six billion people on this planet so there are probably six billion different definitions of exactly what fun is. The activities that a thirty-year-old Democratic web designer from New York considers fun will be much different from that of a sixty-two-year-old Republican farmer from Arizona. Fun is a noun, a verb and an adjective.

The dictionary refers to it as playfulness, merry play or amusement. For me, having fun merely means creating more opportunities to experience joyful feelings. Fun is a way to expand your happiness levels to the maximum. It's an emotional, mental and physical ritual that will bring more joy into your daily life. When you are experiencing fun, you are living in the moment and expressing your spirit to the world. Fun keeps your blood pumping and magnifies your zest for living.

The simplest definition is this: Fun is a way of being. It is a skill that is learned, developed and honed. People who possess a "fun" state of mind just have a flexible way of discovering their world without prejudices or judgment. Fun is being involved in your environment and participating in life. It is not the ultimate destination but a way of traveling down the road. True fun knows no color of skin, any political alliance or religious endeavor. Fun is about you enjoying your life. Whether you play tennis, go shopping or stick carrots up your nose–good for you–whatever makes you happy.

There are certain activities that should never be considered fun under any circumstance.

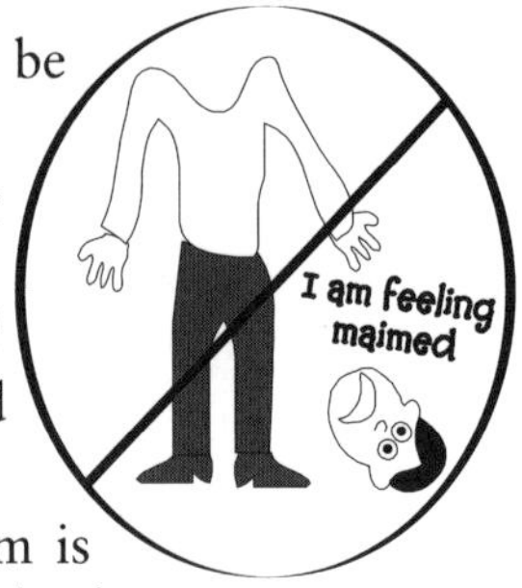

1) Any activity in which human beings are injured or maimed physically, financially, emotionally or mentally without prior approval. Side effects: Guilt, loss of friends, jail time, broken bones, public ridicule and stains on your clothes that never come out.

2) Laughing at people instead of laughing with them is just an uninvited form of abuse. Side effects: Invariably shows that the person doing the attacking has low self-esteem.

3) Doing jobs or activities that you despise. Side effects: Ulcers, stress and anger.

4) Any activity in which animals are injured, maimed or killed for no particular reason. Side effects: You begin to hear barking in the night, but there is no dog there.

So I hope that helps in defining fun, but defining a fun person will also help. In my experiences with fun people, I've always wondered how they can wake up with a giggle and a smile no matter what's going on in their lives. I had to know the who's, why's, where's, what's and how's of fun, and this is what I found.

I discovered that no one kind of person is more deserving or more likely to be fun than another. They can be rich or poor, good-looking or funny-looking. They were not confined to a certain age, culture, religion, location or ethnic group.

The one common thread these people possess in their lives is a fun way of thinking–a belief system that helps them perceive the world in a way that's beneficial to their level of happiness. They have their share of misery and woe. They get angry, they cry, become scared, get jealous and encounter bad situations. Instead of dwelling in the negative, however, they immediately start to think of the positive. They understand that there is little or no value in wasting your attention and energy on something that makes you feel like crap.

Fun people have the ability to enjoy whatever life throws at them. If their house burns down, they say, "Gosh, am I glad I'm not on fire." They lose their job and all they can think about is what's next? When they get dumped, they rejoice because they have learned some lessons and can now move on to find someone who is a better match. The flat tire in the middle of nowhere isn't bad luck, it's an exciting adventure. When they realize they are burdened with negative emotions, they know how to move on and get doing the things they enjoy doing.

Chuckle-chasers understand that fun is a necessary part of a balanced life. They live in the moment and for the moment. They learn from the past, enjoy the present and dream about the future. They may use alcohol or stimulants, but they aren't a necessity for having fun. They don't want to escape the moment–they want to live in it.

All we are is the result of what we have thought.
Buddha

Giggle-getters are committed to pursuing activities that bring them joy. Regardless of what is going on in their lives, they still find the time to get out and get pleasure from the world. They usually have a fulfilling career and a reasonable lifestyle. Having nice things around them is important to them, but it is not an obsession.

Lovers of fun understand that their brain is the part of their body that makes them happy. They challenge their brain and fill it up with new ideas and concepts. Through flexible thinking and the process of gaining more knowledge, they achieve a sense of freedom.

These lovers of life find it easy to be pleased about a tree, a bird, a flower, a good friend, a great piece of pie or a colorful sunset. Happy people go into life with open ears, eyes, hearts and minds. They are curious about the people around them and seem to respect the planet and the creatures of it. They realize that the world is always morphing and changing, and as a human being they need to transform as well.

Fun people have many childlike qualities, like playfulness and curiosity. They are quick to laugh–at the world around them and at themselves. They say yes to new adventures and new experiences. Fun people do not set unrealistic expectations for themselves, the people around them or the events in their lives. They expect to enjoy themselves no matter what happens.

When they play in life, they give it their best but know that winning is not the most important part. They are more concerned about giving a good effort and enjoying the game. They know that high fitness levels keep them feeling good. These fun worshippers understand that their bodies are the apparatus that allows them to move around to discover life, so they take care of that apparatus. Yes, they eat chocolate and hamburgers and ice cream, but they do it in moderation. When they have exhausted their energy reserves, they know how and when to relax.

Happiness hounds are not interested in sensational news coverage. Their days are not dictated by how many people died and for what reasons. They are sympathetic to the troubles of the world, but they are unwilling to let all of the world's woes affect their lives. They watch very little TV because they're too busy enjoying life. Instead of seeing what is wrong with the world they are out there experiencing what is right.

Getting there isn't half the fun - it's all the fun. Robert Townsend

They have high standards in all of their relationships. Whether it is business or personal, they rarely have people in their lives who cause them grief. Fun people realize that compromising your spirit for a better deal, higher social status or a little sexual action just isn't worth it. They have learned how to say no to activities or people that take them away from happiness. They do not depend on their friends or lovers to make them complete and happy–they just have them around to help achieve that happiness.

They have careers that challenge them and get them out of bed in the morning. If they hate their jobs, they're actively working on a day-to-day basis towards a more satisfying profession. Fun people have excellent control over their time, their money and their energy. They understand that there needs to be a balance between work, play, family and friends. They seem to have a certain wisdom in prioritizing where fun fits into the picture.

I can tell you that my own personal pursuit of fun has shown me that a true endorphin high comes from that blissful state of fun. The more I experience life, the more I have realized that fun is an addiction all in itself. And what a wonderful addiction it is. Now that you have a target to aim for, the question is: How can you discover more fun in your life?

May the spirit of happiness fly up your nose. Terry Dolle

Who and Why?

Nobody really cares if you are miserable,
so you might as well be happy.
Cythina Nelms

All kinds of research has been done to see if certain kinds of people have more fun than others. The results? No particular kind of person is prone to more fun. There are lots of happy poor people and plenty of dissatisfied rich people. Race, political or religious beliefs, boy or girl, it just doesn't seem to matter. First-world country or third-world country will have an effect, but there are plenty of happy people without three TVs and twenty pairs of shoes. It doesn't matter who you are, how intelligent you are or where you live, everyone has the ability and is entitled to a life full of joy and happiness.

There isn't any truth to the myth that some people deserve to have fun and some people don't. All of us have had terrible experiences that can affect who we are today. If your list of misfortunes is longer than your neighbor's, it doesn't mean you are less deserving of happiness. In the United States, a citizen's pursuit of happiness is an inalienable right. Why have we lost sight of that right? Can you imagine if lobbyists spent their time pursuing the availability of funs instead of the availability of guns?

Everybody wants to have fun, but very few people experience it on a regular basis. It makes you feel good, recharges your spiritual batteries and gives you more energy in your life. It is far more natural to be happy than to be miserable. Having fun is not an activity that breaks you away from reality; it is a way of living

that helps you deal with reality. There is a common misperception that having fun is an act of self-gratification. It's not. Having fun is your right, and as long as it isn't detrimental to others, it is not self-gratification but an act of living in a joyous manner. Truly having fun is completely underrated and ignored in our society even though we have a natural desire and need for it.

Laughing and having fun helps your body move oxygen and nutrients around, reduces your blood pressure and heart rate and helps you deal with stress. It tightens your abdominal muscles, massages your internal organs, produces more T-cells, helps fight depression, aids digestion, stimulates the immune system and produces natural endorphins that provide a legal high.

Fun speaks all languages and is enjoyed by all humans. Being caught up in the spirit of fun helps you communicate better, lets you laugh at adversity, gain trust more easily and encourages you to bond with others. Frankly, it just makes you more likable, and what could be wrong with that? It will spice up your love life, your friendships and your work environment. Having fun helps you cope more effectively with life's challenges, gives you a positive outlook, helps you tap into your creative self and gets you connected to life. It helps time fly, creates goodwill and, best of all, fun fights boredom. With all those reasons why fun is so groovy, baby, do you think it's worth considering?

There are three kinds of people: those who can count, and those who can't.
Source unknown

Fun is a commodity that is worshipped by some, wished for by many and completely damned by serious people. These stressed-out humans are in every walk of life and every corner of the planet. No matter what the situation is, there will be somebody who takes it too seriously. These poor souls have been sold the bill of goods that says being serious is a great way to live. There are certainly enough moments that call for people to be serious, but most of those moments don't become serious until we decide they should. Perhaps you're thinking, if there are so many serious specimens out there, there must be some advantage to not being fun.

Let's look at some of the benefits of seriousness.

- Can cut down on the Christmas presents you have to buy since seriousness tends to limit the number of friends you have
- Good for serious situations (i.e., car accidents or emergencies)
- Essential if you want people to take you very seriously
- Excellent for creating psychosomatic illnesses
- Great for ulcers, fatigue, headaches frigidity, impotence, excess mucus and wrinkles

Setbacks to Seriousness

This seriousness that society is currently experiencing comes from a long line of serious people with serious upbringings. We're conditioned to seriousness through our culture, our jobs and our education. As we grow older, serious attitudes and beliefs solidify so that we tend to build a serious life with serious friends and serious conversations. Being a fun person does not mean you have to be any less professional in your job or less respected in your community. You're just showing a sparkly side of you that has been repressed.

To have fun, you need to resign from being serious

Oh, you say, but my job is serious. Whatever. There are police officers, paramedics and morticians who see more doom and gloom in a week than you do in a whole year. If you currently have a serious job, you have even more reasons to lighten up. Being a serious, stressed-out soul makes you easy prey for the forces of evil, and God knows we wouldn't want that to happen.

Where did the seriousness come from? It's really hard to pin down, but mostly it came from serious people, generations of them. They've been trying to convince people that laughing, giggling and horseplay are for children with little, undeveloped minds. Serious people try to belittle happy people, calling them weird or silly. Anybody who is having fun out of the serious box is obviously mentally challenged or totally immature.

Instead of enjoying yourself, you should be obsessed with getting more material possessions. More cars, a bigger house, more clothes, whatever. Work more serious hours on serious projects for more stupendously serious results. How many people turn fifty or sixty with a serious amount of material possessions but haven't experienced hardly any fun? They don't even know how to start because their lives have been consumed with acquiring and worrying about all their stuff. When they finally retire, they have lost their health and their youth.

If you are extremely serious, you may find yourself extremely unhappy. Just lighten up a little bit, just a pinch, it's OK. Your mission is not to accomplish everything in life; it is about enjoying life no matter what happens. It's not the person with the most toys who wins; it's the person with the most joys who wins. You are ultimately responsible for whether you have a good time on earth or not.

You have reached a major achievement by reading this book this far and not throwing it at the wall in a cussing seizure. We have more or less defined fun and that it probably is good for you. Next we're going to look at some of the excuses people use to avoid having fun.

If you can learn to smile at whatever curveball has been thrown at you, you have discovered true success in life. Schredd

Excuses

Don't tell me why you can't, tell me how you can. Robert G. Ivanco

Excuses stop you from having more fun, more love and more good times in your life. That's the only thing they do. We're presented with unlimited opportunities to do, see and experience life. Go here, go there, go everywhere. The problem is we just can't do everything so we say no to plenty of potential joy.

Here are the most popular fun-avoiding excuses:

Excuse Number One: I'm too old for that. You are never too old to enjoy anything; you will just enjoy different things. Besides, when exactly does "too old" take place? At twenty, thirty, forty, fifty, sixty, seventy? There are seventy-year-old triathletes, skydivers, university students and mountain climbers. Look, there are senior citizens kicking butt all over the planet. Don't let your butt be on the receiving end of those kicks. You are only too old when you're dead.

Old age is an excellent time for outrage. My goal is to say or do at least one outrageous thing every week. Maggie Kuhn

Excuse Number Two: My health is no good so I'm unable to participate. Well, tell that to cancer survivor Lance Armstrong after he won the Tour de France. If you stop living because of your perceived restrictions, you are the only loser. Fun people say regardless of what ails me I am going to give it a go. They don't believe physical ailments or disabilities will hold them back.

Excuse Number Three: I don't deserve it. Is this a ridiculous excuse or is it just me? Of course you deserve to have some fun, and a lot of it.

Excuse Number Four: It's too dangerous. Compared to what? Crossing the street? Eating at a greasy spoon? Everything has an element of danger to it. If you love to make the worst-case scenario in your head eventually you will be lonely, bored and dead.

Excuse Number Five: I've never tried . . . walking on hot coals, Argentinian tango, speaking Norwegian, riding a camel or acting on stage and I don't want to look stupid trying something I've never done before. Every minute of every day, somebody, somewhere is doing something they've never done before, just once. Oddly enough, it's the only way to try something new.

Excuse Number Six: I don't have the time. Everybody has the same amount of time. It's just how people use it. If you say you have no time for fun, then you just haven't made fun a priority.

Excuse Number Seven: It costs too much. There are plenty of activities that cost next to nothing: a picnic at the park, a walk by a lake, a romp at the playground or a smooch with a special friend. If you really have your heart set on an expensive activity, all you have to do is ask what will it take for this to happen? Could you get a part-time job, trade some service you can perform with someone else, borrow the equipment, buy the equipment second-hand? Don't shut down a possibility because it's too expensive. Instead of saying "no" just ask "how?"

Excuse Number Eight: I won't know anybody. You don't know anybody, so you stay home, which helps you to solidify your belief that you don't know anybody. Fun practitioners are excited to meet new people. Maybe they can add to their list of playmates. The only way you get to know people is to get to know people.

Excuse Number Nine through Twenty-six: Life is supposed to be a struggle. That's childish. My dog wouldn't approve. I have to do it the old way. But the animals will get me. You need special training for that. They don't sell pork there. I can't play with them because they're a different religion. I would but I'm just too fat. I'm too scared. I smell. The weather is always bad. If only I had a million dollars, then I could have some fun. I don't have the right clothes. I might hurt myself. Someone might laugh at me. Or whatever other excuse works for you.

He that is good for making excuses is seldom good for anything else. Benjamin Franklin

Excuses seem perfectly valid in the eyes of those who create them, but in reality they're ridiculous. When you use excuses, you repel the very fun people and situations that can bring you happiness. If you truly believe you're too old, what do you think will happen? You're just going to get older and older. If you've decided you don't want to feel stupid trying a new activity, then why bother trying it in the first place, right?

A man can fail many times, but he isn't a failure until he begins to blame somebody else. John Burroughs

Eventually your excuses will solidify into beliefs and, unfortunately, changing your beliefs is a little more challenging. Best to nip this situation in the bud before the excuses harden into beliefs. So how the heck does one stop this chronic excuse thing?

Begin by admitting the truth–you are responsible for the level of fun in your life. Everything that is around you–your house, your lovers, your job and your circumstances–is a direct result of you and the way you think. So many people look outside themselves to blame or excuse themselves from their reality, but it takes courage for people to accept responsibility.

Avoiding responsibility by making excuses takes away your personal power and leaves you open to further anxieties. Blaming somebody or some entity will NEVER solve the problem. Blame the world, blame the government, blame the farmers, blame the little goat at the zoo–it's all their fault. Anything, any statement to deflect the real root of the problem. To think that other people or the government are responsible for fixing your life is silly. It only prolongs the inevitable fact that only you can make your life great, fun and delicious.

The great leaders in history were always able to take responsibility. Unfortunately, there have not been that many great leaders. Most leaders these days just deny and deflect responsibility. They use a political sleight of hand to retain their power and put the focus somewhere else. It was the Republicans, the Democrats, the economy, the weather, the local government, the FBI, the police, the whites, the blacks and on and on. We have very few responsible role models in our political system. It seems as if the only people in our society who think they don't need to take responsibility are the politicians and the celebrities.

Our culture rewards lack of responsibility. Do you remember the case of the "I drank hot coffee and I'm suing McDonald's"? Somebody went to McDonald's, ordered a coffee, drank it and found it was too hot. So they decided to sue McDonald's. Isn't coffee supposed to be hot?

What about a woman who sued Universal Studios because, she said, the theme park Halloween Horror Nights Haunted House was too scary for her and caused her emotional distress. In a different pitiful example of responsibility avoidance, the family of a man who drowned on a fishing trip sued the Weather Channel for ten million dollars claiming that the man was tricked by the station's storm-free forecast. At Disneyland, a man drove into his fiancée on the bumper car ride. The injured woman then sued Disneyland and her own fiancée. OK, just one more. Some people have a party. Guests come over and drink. The hosts offer a free cab ride but the drunken visitor refuses. Mr. Party Pants decides to drive, crashes his car, blames the hosts and sues.

Yes, there are plenty of situations where companies or individuals need to be punished for unacceptable behavior.

But the coffee is too hot? The Halloween night is too scary? The weather forecast is wrong? The bumper cars are too bumpery? Oh my God, that's terrible. You must get a lawyer and sue. The lawyers and litigants in these frivolous lawsuits should be given a slap upside the head and a stupid ticket. I don't understand why they haven't tried to sue God for making the cliffs too cliffy and the tornadoes too twisty. The media helps out by highlighting these stories of ridiculous litigation. Their barrage of "blame experts" can find fault with anyone and anything. We being the information sponges that we are believe them word for word. Then it sets off a frenzy of copycat litigation. If they can sue over hot coffee, what could I sue for? When people are truly responsible, they can't admit it for fear of being sued. If we can't take responsibility for drinking coffee that's too hot for us, then how can we ever take responsibility for our own happiness?

You have the choice to take responsibility for your life. You are wherever you are in this moment in your life because you brought yourself there. Evaluate your job, your friends, your lovers or lack of, where you have been and where you are going. You created it all. Good or bad, you are responsible. Then imagine where you would like to go. Then think of all the excuses you have used in the past. Taking responsibility allows you the freedom to grow. No excuse can ever justify you not discovering, exploring, adventuring, laughing and enjoying your life. There are more than enough roadblocks to happiness in your life. Why ensure that it won't happen with the habitual use of excuses?

A bad workman always blames his tools. Proverb

Mind Poo

In the long run, the pessimist may be proven right,
but the optimist has a better time on the trip.
Daniel Readon

Have you ever been out in the world and some person or event sends you into a flying hag bag of negative emotions? Or you feel overwhelmed with downbeat thoughts like anger, fear, sadness and all of their cousins, namely guilt, jealousy, revenge and manipulation? This is what my Grandma Schredd called Mind Poo. Mind Poo distorts your perceptions, affects your actions and destroys whatever glimmers of happiness or fun that have found their way to you. Maybe you're angry during your commute, scared about the state of the world or sad because of some terrible event. So often we pretend these rotten feelings don't exist and then we store them as bad vibes in our bodies.

USE REPEATEDLY FOR SEVERE DAMAGE

When you buy into these thoughts, your emotions get involved and that's when it gets ugly. Mind Poo will keep your shoulders tense, your chest tight, provide plenty of headaches, anxiety attacks and tension in the jaw. Look for all kinds of bonus diseases like cancer or depression. It can impair your concentration and create a barrage of harsh negative statements. It will affect your sleeping patterns and your appetite. Mind Poo also encourages isolation, thereby boosting your alcohol or drug intake and increasing your craving for junk food. In extreme cases, it may leave you feeling overwhelmed, hopeless and suicidal. Mind Poo makes it very difficult to smile, giggle or laugh.

Take a look at the people around you. Do they beam? Do you see a glow? Or do they look a little dull? If you look deep into their eyes, you can actually see whether they're angry, scared, sad, neutral or glad. Look at yourself in the mirror–not a glance but an honest evaluation. What do you see? Is there a shade of Mind Poo there? Don't worry, it's not the real you.

Where does the Mind Poo come from? Imagine your body is a radio receiver. There are heaps of radio stations you can tune into. Some are fantastic spiritual stations like joy, fun and love. You can tune into negative stations like anger, sadness, fear or guilt. Depending on where you are, some stations broadcast at a stronger signal than others. All these stations are broadcasting twenty-four hours a day, seven days a week.

Once you discover you're tuned into the wrong station, how do you turn the dial? It begins when you realize that the Mind Poo never was you, it never has been you and it never will be you. Hallelujah. You will experience anger, fear, sadness, guilt and a host of other negative emotions, but they are not you. They are just bad radio signals that exist and weave their way through every corner of the planet.

A positive attitude gets you farther than a negative one. Oh, good posture and smiling helps too.
Cory Brooke Young

Turning off the Mind Poo doesn't mean the bad stations aren't broadcasting, it just means you have tuned out the signal. All you have to do is learn how to spin the dial when you've made the wrong selection. Everybody tunes into Mind Poo every now and then. It's just a matter of how long you keep listening. Be aware of the triggers that change the radio station from love and joy to ticked off and angry. A car cuts you off in traffic; the kids don't hang up their jackets; the phone company overcharges you. Regular day-to-day things can tweak you into Mind Poo radio, but you don't have to listen.

When you become stuck in Mind Poo, it can be very difficult to get out of it. Your perception of problems becomes so distorted you believe you have no control over your life. Mind Poo loves to impose imagined barriers on you that don't exist in reality. Dealing with your Mind Poo is like being an athlete. During the training process, you may experience challenge, pain and suffering. Through this method, you gain physical fitness and a sense of well-being. Working through Mind Poo may be a little challenging, but eventually it will greatly improve your day-to-day happiness levels.

Happy Harold decided not to listen to the Mind Poo

Mind Poo is like the pain you get when you stick your hand in a fire. It lets you know that you need to attend to a problem–like getting your bubbling hand out of there. Instead of a burnt hand, your problem may be addressing situations where patience, courage, compassion, self-esteem, love, kindness or strength are the remedies. If your Mind Poo goes untreated, it will eventually consume you, festering inside your body and controlling your innate ability to enjoy life. In the following chapters, we'll look at the different flavors of Mind Poo.

Optimism is the cheerful frame of mind that enables a tea kettle to sing, though it's in hot water up to its nose.
Unknown

Anger

Anger is an acid that can do more harm to the vessel in which it is stored than to anything on which it is poured.
Source unknown

Everybody tunes into anger radio on a fairly regular basis. It may be subtle or it could be full-blown rage. Our fast-paced society gives us numerous things to make our ears tingle. We get miffed because it rains on our day off, somebody is late to pick us up, a dorky co-worker gets a promotion, the computer crashes or the waiter brings cold soup. We get mad at our parents, our lover, our friends or the government. When you're a cranky-pants, you cannot have fun. It's impossible.

The World Sucks MmmKay...

Anger causes raised voices, temper tantrums, arguments, physical violence and regrettable actions. It strains your heart and raises your blood pressure. It will cloud your judgment and wreak havoc on your personal relationships. You can become so irate that you're unable to think or act in a rational manner. You can get so furious that your face becomes contorted and ugly. We mentally multiply our rage and make it bigger than it needs to be. When your anger goes unchecked, it begins to fester and bubble like a giant pimple. When it finally erupts, it's painful and messy. Anger breeds anger.

Angry Andy

When we get in a huff, we will take it out on others. Then feelings are hurt and hearts are broken. When your blood is boiling and you let an unsuspecting person feel your wrath, you're doing a disservice to humanity. Whether we're on the giving or receiving end of rage, none of us walks out of there with smiles on our faces.

Not Angry Andy

When we get mad, we think our being angry will somehow make the person who is responsible suffer. The person you're mad at rarely suffers. Most of the time they don't even know you exist. So, while they're busy not suffering, that anger is shared with everyone else in the world. We lash out at people who have nothing to do with why we are livid in the first place. When you "lose it," you become poison to yourself and everybody within earshot. It takes only seconds to open a wound but it may take years to heal it.

A textbook example of taking your anger out on somebody who doesn't deserve it

The essence of anger instigation is when we try to change something that's impossible to change. If you got a parking ticket today, it isn't going to change by yelling profanities. Getting mad at the government because of financial policies will not change the economy. Getting hot under the collar at your late taxi will not set the clocks back. Foaming at the mouth because your car won't start will only create foam. All you can do is embrace what has happened. You can either blow your top or let it slide. You only become irate when acceptance of the situation is denied.

A winner rebukes and forgives; a loser is too timid to rebuke and too petty to forgive. Sidney J. Harris

Bad things happen and they happen all the time. There will always be pain, misfortune, civil authority and people who will make your blood boil. Nobody on the planet is free from unpleasant experiences. If you can realistically do something to change the problem, then all the power to you. If you can't, then let it slide. Let it slide past first, second, third and home. If you stay angry, all you do is carry around feelings of ill will. It doesn't make any sense to waste your time or energy being angry.

We generalize the problem and blame all women, all men, all whites, all blacks, the Muslims, the Catholics, the Protestants, or whichever brand of people has harmed us in the past. When generalized anger continues to be developed and nurtured, it turns into hatred. Hatred has no other role than to cause harm.

Once it gets to this stage, it is very difficult to get back to a neutral, never mind an accepting state. People lash out and take revenge to justify all this bitter resentment they're carrying around. When you seek payback on someone and make them suffer, what is there to be happy about?

Another anger trigger is the need to be right. Sometimes it's nice to be right, but shoving your point of view down people's throats isn't going to make your life any easier. What is your ultimate goal: to make everybody resent your righteousness or get along with those around you? Remember, you'll catch a lot more flies using honey instead of vinegar.

I will never understand why people choose being right over being happy. In Ireland, it is the Catholics against the Protestants. Or it might be the Palestinians against Israelis. Or maybe it is a right/wrong from the past. Slavery or treatment of the Aboriginals. The terrorists against the US. All this time and energy, lives lost and freedoms restricted-all because each side of this disagreement is more interested in shouting their point of view to the world than living a normal life or trying to understand the people on the other side of the fence. They are destroying their own lives in the process and teaching children to hate. Why? Because they prefer to be right, to pursue justice, than to pursue peace and happiness.

Whenever two groups argue to prove who is right, it is very difficult to ever come to a resolution. It is such a sad scenario when families break up, lovers are lost and friendships dissolve, all because somebody had to be right. In these little disagreements, people become more concerned about who's right and not what's right. Look for resolution or solution so you can spend your time enjoying your life.

Anger is a momentary madness, so control your passion or it will control you. Horace

The Dalai Lama has a wonderful theory on how to deal with people and situations that make you angry. When His Holiness is confronted with a possible anger stimulant, he becomes excited: A teacher has arrived to teach him the valuable lessons of patience and tolerance. But what if this person is trying to hurt you? Why would you want to be grateful? There are plenty of people who we feel want to harm us–like the dentist and his giant drill or the fitness instructor who makes us do those last ten push-ups. You understand the benefit of the evil dentist and the heartless fitness instructor. So, these people who get you angry or cause mental pain are really helping you to become a better person, a more patient person. I found this theory so profound that it changed the way I look at anger forever.

When you're angry with someone, you may perceive him or her to be a really nasty specimen of a human. But maybe it isn't true. Whether they have done something to you on purpose or by accident, it is not a reflection of their whole personality. There are probably plenty of wonderful traits this person has that you are either forgetting about or don't know exist. If you focus on what is good about the person, you will find your anger beginning to disappear. If you can find nothing positive, just let it go. Forget about it and get on with your life.

If you need to get angry, do it once, not over and over like a broken record. You may feel energized when you free that anger from your system. Sometimes just talking about it helps, or try deep breathing and count to ten. If it's a big problem, you may have to count to a hundred, or maybe use a punching bag. Maybe you need to go throw a rock or yell at a tree. If anger becomes tightly woven into your personality, go seek some professional help.

You cannot shake hands with a clenched fist. Indira Gandhi

Practice anger intervention at its smallest level because when it gets big you could truly go postal over the most inconsequential event. Forgive yourself, forgive your parents, forgive what you need to forgive and let it go. If you want to get revenge on your enemies, just forgive them. That will drive them crazy. Accept the past. Whatever happened has already happened. Learn from the situation and move on.

Properly directed anger can be highly motivational, but if it's not dealt with it will be devastating to you emotionally, mentally and physically. If something is bothering you, then make a phone call, write a letter or talk to a friend. Some form of gentle expression of your anger will help to solve the problem. Try fast walking, jogging, crazy dancing or any other activity that helps you release that anger by moving energy through your body. You don't need to remain angry to cause change in the world.

To carry a grudge is like being stung to death by one bee
WILLIAM H. WALTON

If you find yourself in an angry situation, ask, "If I were Mother Teresa, the Dalai Lama or Jesus, what would I do in this situation?" Can you imagine the Dalai Lama at the counter demanding customer service? Can you see Mother Teresa racing after someone who had just cut her off in traffic? Do you think Jesus got into fistfights about what tasted better–broccoli or corn? These people didn't get angry about the problems of the world. They were, and in the Dalai Lama's case are, too busy working towards doing something about them.

Not only do we need to let things slide, we need to stop looking for opportunities to get mad. Some of us (not you, of course, I mean the "others") create situations that set them off. For example, we'll be driving down the road waiting for the opportunity for people to screw up so we can honk or yell at them. We see another car in the next lane, know he has to get in our lane and we speed up so he can't get in. Then we get mad when he cuts us off. We could have just let him in, made him happy and gone on our way. Why put extra effort into creating situations that make us snap? Stop looking for people to get upset at and start looking for ways to let it slide.

You probably don't have tons of enemies and the world is not out to do you harm, but if you have some form of anger it will stick you in the gizzard all day long. The easiest way to dissipate anger is to let it go. Calm down and chill out. Will this really matter to you a year from now? How about one month? A week? One day? One hour? Think forgiveness and acceptance. If you want to have a happy life, minimize your need to be right. You don't have to win an argument to win an argument. It's like wrestling with a pig. You both get filthy and chances are, the pig will enjoy it. Let the pig win. Why get angry when you can get fun?

A chip on the shoulder indicates there is wood higher up.
Jack Herbert

Fear

He without benefit of scruples, his fun and money soon quadruples. Ogden Nash

Fear scares people. That's what it's supposed to do; it's just a matter of how much and how often do we really need to be scared? Basically, there are two kinds of fear. Real fear allows you to save your butt in challenging situations (like being chased by a predator or facing imminent danger). Then there are imagined fears–which hold you back from experiencing life. Imagined fears may come from a previous unpleasant experience, other people's fears or bad information. The way your brain sees it there is no difference between an imaginary fear and a real one.

Fear can provide stress and physical anxiety as you prepare for new experiences. It can cause you to lack good judgment or to do irrational things. Chicken-heartedness can turn into terror and complete immobilization. Or you can change your panic into an exciting edge when stepping out of your comfort zone. What's scary for some is sheer delight for others. Confronting your fears will give you an incredible sense of satisfaction and confidence.

Your happiness is directly related to whether fear runs your activity schedule or your courage does. In a modern world, fear has minimal uses, especially if the perceived concern has no basis in reality. When you are full of fear, you end up worrying about events that will never even happen. We worry about the environment, the safety of the neighborhood or world peace. We worry about murderers, terrorists and the stock markets. Some people call it worrying; others call it being realistic. But worrying is a waste of time; it has never paid a single bill nor stopped a hurricane. If the situation or problem can be remedied, there is no point worrying about it. If there is nothing you can do about your problems, there is no point worrying either.

Fear makes the wolf bigger than he is. German proverb

Think about the fears and worries in your life and how they affect your fun level. You don't have to deny your fears, just question if they're truly looking out for your best interests. Are you focusing on what could go wrong instead of what could go right? So many people are consumed by worry, hoping that one day their lives will get better, as another day slips away. Instead of seeing the worst-case scenario in your mind, see the best-case scenario. Become what motivational speaker Brian Tracey calls an inverse paranoid. Become convinced that there are of people waiting around every corner to show you some form of fun or pleasure. Become paranoid that the world is out to do you good.

Now, fun people do not deny their fears. Are they scared when they face their fears? You bet, but devoted delight detectors make it a habit of facing their fears instead of tucking their tails behind their legs and hiding under the bed. They change their fears from a debilitating annoyance into waves of adrenaline and excitement. When you face your fears, whether you succeed or not, you are a winner. You are a winner because you have chosen to be motivated by your passion for living and not by fear.

The way to counteract your fears and worries is to gain knowledge, which gives you courage. Use wisdom, not worries, when traipsing out into the world. If you were to head out hiking in the mountains, would you worry that you could fall off a cliff, become lost, get eaten by a bear or get hit by an avalanche? These are all possible scenarios, but only remotely possible. The more you worry about it, the more likely you are to create it. If you stay away from the cliffs, take a map and a compass, avoid taping salmon to your body and stay out of the avalanche zones, you'll be fine.

Do the thing you fear to do and keep on doing it ... that is the quickest way ever discovered to conquer fear. Dale Carnegie

The wrong vision

We do so many dangerous things in our everyday lives and yet we worry about a little adventure. What about crossing the street? Do you see yourself getting pegged by a bus? Of course you don't. So when we consider new or unknown activities, why do we create such terrible visions? Chances for a major injury are much greater crossing a busy street than traipsing in the mountains. If something does happen while you're enjoying the world, at least you're living! Watching TV and eating potato chips may be safe but you will get fat and it's boring.

If you say no to snorkeling in the ocean because you're scared of sharks or sea monsters, you're the one who loses. You will never see the magic of the underwater world. Yes, there is that chance that a water monster might go for a snack while you're splashing around, but the chances are so slim. You have a better chance of being hit by lightning or winning an Olympic gold medal. Thousands if not millions of people have been in the ocean and survived. Why would you be singled out for tragedy?

Anything I've ever done that ultimately was worthwhile. initially scared me to death. Betty Bender

You will never be able to remove every potential danger, but you can diminish the threat by following the golden rule of adventure: safety first. If there's a way to lower the risk factor, do it. If there's protective gear, wear it. If there's a need for common sense, then use it. Take the proper steps to ensure your safety. Do you need a life jacket, a helmet or special training before you try this activity? What about learning from a professional? Yes, every year, a few people die while they're out having fun, but often that's because they haven't been smart about safety precautions. So be smart. Dying because of stupidity makes you stupid and dead. And being both dead AND stupid is definitely embarrassing. Avoid it at all costs.

Let's say you want to go kayaking. Kayaking is a much more enjoyable experience if you know how to swim and how to self-rescue. Learning to minimize the danger of any activity will help you face the world. The more you understand something, the less you will fear it. The more people you meet who are doing that activity, the more confidence you'll have in saying, "They're no better than me–I can do this!" You may find that this activity you've perceived as treacherous isn't that dangerous after all.

So you've gained some knowledge and you've made arrangements for a safe experience, but you're still too scared to get on the roller coaster or get out on the dance floor. Then turn your fear into excitement. Feel the fear and do it anyway. Be thankful that you have this highly tuned system that recognizes danger and lets your senses sharpen. Let it send tingles to the tips of your toes and enjoy the burst of energy. Fear will multiply your excitement sensations. You may be scared now, but when you come out the other side, you will feel fantastic, confident, proud and reliving your wonderful adventure. Another positive twist on being scared is that the more scared you are, the more intense your pleasure will be during and after your fun activity.

Considering how dangerous everything is,
nothing is really very frightening. Gertrude Stein

Most of your fears are imagined and should be treated as imaginary. Learn to distinguish the fears that are valid and those that are not. The next time you feel scared, confront your fear and the thing you fear will disappear. Ask yourself, "What would I be doing if I wasn't feeling fear?" then act accordingly. When you confront your fears, astonishing things will happen. Remember you are the master and you are in control.

Just because you are paranoid doesn't mean they're not after you. Kurt Cobain

Each time you challenge your fears, you add another brick to a solid foundation for happiness. Each tiny little fear that you face and conquer will give you courage against all your other fears. If you're unable to take control of your fears or have some kind of panic disorder, go and seek professional help. Moving past unreasonable fears will give you astonishing amounts of self-respect, confidence and satisfaction. Use courage and knowledge to assist you in your journey. If there is a fun activity that you want to try but are afraid, make a plan to conquer your fears. Investigate it, take some lessons, learn what you can, turn your fear into excitement, pretend to be brave and then go for it. Who runs your life, unfounded fears or wonderful you?

Paralyze resistance with persistence

WOODY HAYES

The experience of conquering your fears is so freeing and such a confidence builder that every fear-busting experience is worth it.
Charles H. Givens

Sadness

The young man who has not wept is a savage, and the old man who will not laugh is a fool. George Santayana

Sadness is the body's way of telling you how much it misses being happy. Relationships end, jobs are lost, people die, welcome to the game of life. Sadness is a natural reaction to a loss of some kind. Every person on the planet has situations that can bring on sadness. It can be loneliness, someone else's misery or an unexpected event that brings on a state of doom and gloom.

As a kind, compassionate human, it is easy to become sad because of the state of the world. We know that people are dying from starvation. There is a suicide attempt every minute in the U.S. We are poisoning our water, our land and our air. Animals are being abused. Teenagers get pregnant, street people are addicted to drugs and school kids are getting shot in their classrooms. What are you going to do? Being sad will do nothing to change these problems. Remaining sad is extremely toxic to your system and to those around you.

If you dwell on problems long enough, it just solidifies them. Moping around like Eeyore is never going to cheer you up. You may feel justified in having the blues, but not only do you suffer, your low spirits affect everyone you meet. When you are heavy-hearted, it is common to search out people to agree with you and your problems. Instead of looking for solutions, you are just emphasizing your doldrums.

If someone else is overwhelmed with sadness, they begin to suck your energy. You know the people who seem to dwell on their troubles. Whether it's a sibling, a friend or the guy at the corner store, reinforcing their problems will not help them. They prefer it when the world agrees with their "my life sucks" theories. Yes, they will get attention, but it's short-lived and does nothing to solve their problems. If you're there when they're sharing sadness, there's a good chance it will stick to you. Do the best you can to cheer them up and move on when you need to.

Fun people have compassion for the problems of the world, but they aren't busy being sad about them either. The only way to deal with your sadness is to proactively do something about it. You don't have to pretend you're not despondent, but I do recommend trying to put your sadness into perspective. If you're having a run of bad luck, the more focus you give your problems the more intense they will become. Feeling sorry for yourself is of no benefit. No matter how bad you think your life may be, there is always somebody who has it worse off than you. If everybody has somebody who's worse off than they are, that leaves one person on the whole planet who is actually the "Worst Off." That "Worst Off" person isn't you, so let's move on.

It's normal to be sad at different stages of your life. It's so abnormal to stay that way. If you have stored-up tears, don't be afraid of crying. Everybody dampens a pillow sometime. Your life may seem so awful that you couldn't have made it up if you'd tried. What if you are knee-deep in cow dung? Do you tell everyone you're stuck or do you ask for help out of the poop? Being sad is like storing dead rats in your refrigerator. If you ever get some fresh fruits and vegetables, it's impossible to fit the new groceries in.

My good friend Kevin has a wonderful perspective on sadness. If he's sad, it makes him happy. His theory is that if he's sad it means he's missing something that once made him very happy. He relates back to those happy thoughts and focuses on them. He realizes why he's sad, enjoys that, sheds a tear and it's over.

If you know someone who tries to drown their sorrows, you might tell them sorrows know how to swim. Anonymous

Identify the situations and people that trigger you to feel sad. If you have chronically heavy-hearted people around you, it is going to be very difficult for you to stay positive. If you are sick and tired of listening to a Mr. or Mrs. Pouty Pants, say to them, "It's your life. What are you going to do about it?" They will either look for a solution or threaten you. "You better listen to my problems," they'll say, "or I'll go somewhere else to whine." Oh, wouldn't that be awful. Unless you're a paid therapist, let them go find somewhere else to whinge about their problems.

Stop doing the activities that bum you out. If staying at home and watching TV depresses you, then stop. If you're playing with people who depress you, then stop! If overeating makes you despondent, then stop! Focus on the activities and people that inspire you to happiness. Talk to jovial humans who uplift and recharge your spirit. Get involved in activities that cheer you up. Having fun is the greatest way to counteract sadness.

If that doesn't work, go help some people who are not as fortunate as you. Making someone else feel good will help put your life into perspective and remind you that your problems are inconsequential in the big picture.

When confronted by challenges, look for solutions, not different angles to bitch about. Moaning and complaining will just make you bitter. If you view your situation as hopeless, you'll be right. If you think you can solve the situation, you'll also be right. It's OK to be sad now and then; it's how you deal with it that reflects who you really are. Some people learn from sadness and move on. Some people stay tuned into sadness for years.

Once you stop performing activities that put you down in the dumps, the way to get happy again is to go have some fun. Go out with your friends, go on an adventure, buy yourself something that makes you feel good. When I say "feel good," I don't mean resorting to addictive behavior like drinking, taking drugs or manic shopping to mask your problems. It's OK to indulge a little, though, to help erase that nasty Mind Poo.

Sadness is the body's way of telling you how much you miss being happy. Think of it as an alarm system that goes off when you're not getting your share of good times. Fight sadness with positive actions. You can remain unhappy and reinforce your sadness or you can ask yourself, "Which way to gladness?"

If you want a rainbow, you have to put up with the rain.
Dolly Parton

Guilt

Each snowflake in an avalanche pleads not guilty.
J. Lec Stanislaw

Everybody has done something wrong in his or her life–no one is excluded. You will miss appointments or birthdays, cheat on your taxes or call your lover a smelly monkey. When we judge our actions as an irreparable mistake, that's when the guilt gang moves in. Accept that you are not perfect, that you will make lapses in judgment.

WHAT GUILT REALLY LOOKS LIKE

Guilt is a nasty little feller that has evolved over time. Whether it's the result of religion or our culture, we have become conditioned to experience guilt on a regular basis. In the hands of the church or the government, guilt can be used to make people feel terrible for events of the past. People in power love to use guilt as a weapon to subdue others. Religion uses it when you begin to even think about questioning the scriptures. Like you're a bad person if you fail to accept every single thing they say. If you break a rule, you have been corrupted by Satan and should feel lousy for at least thirty-seven days and seventy-four nights. On a personal level, guilt can trick us into feeling responsible for problems around the planet. Your feeling guilty does not help starvation and war. They are only helped by you taking some form of positive action. Guilt's most common occupation is as a negative motivator.

There are two reasons to feel guilty. The first reason that you feel guilty is because–you are. Maybe you didn't call or visit when you were supposed to. Or maybe you did commit some form of terrible act like malicious fraud or impaired driving causing injury. If you feel guilty, deal with it by taking ownership of your actions. Then ...

- Regret your actions.
- Apologize to the person(s) you have wronged.
- Try to make it up to them. If you have killed them in a car accident, then it might be a little difficult. Do the best you can.
- Then vow to change yourself so that this situation never happens again.

Taking responsibility with a feeling of remorse is the best way to deal with guilt. Step up to the plate and get what is coming to you. Of course you're going to screw up once in a while, but if you take sincere action to remedy your ways, it will help you to avoid that lapse of good judgment in the future. People make mistakes and, yes, you can do your very best to right your wrongs.

Now the other kind of guilt is fake guilt. Fake guilt or feeling guilty is not the same as being guilty. Fake guilt does nothing but cause needless misery in the world. Feeling fake guilt is a choice. Some religions are quite fanatical about the practice of guilt. If you don't follow these here rules that these "wise" dudes made up a few years back, then you should really feel like crap. That's silly. What kind of an all-loving God would create such beautiful living things and fill them up with guilt? Over punishing yourself with a massive guilt trip will not help you or score a redemption touchdown with the big guy. You created those feelings of fake guilt, so why not minimize them? Maybe you did make an error, but don't beat yourself up for more than your wrong actually merits.

WHAT GUILT DOES

Sometimes life will give us a situation that's out of our control, but we still feel responsible for it. You may feel bad because you were late for an

Whoever blushes confesses guilt, true innocence never feels shame. Jean Jacques Rousseau appointment by an hour and a half because the bus broke down. If somebody gets into a car accident on the way to the grocery store and you were the one who sent him for milk, you might take it personally. What we need is some training on how to feel good. Start by refusing to feel guilty for situations that are out of your hands.

There are plenty of unpleasant circumstances that seem like no-win situations. You have to fire an employee or break up with a lover. Maybe you ran over the neighbor's cat. What if you have to kill someone in self-defense or in a war? Do your best to deal with it. Help that employee find a new job, tell your lover it wasn't their fault, it was yours, and take kitty to the vet or get your neighbor a new one when the time is right. You may be saddened by this unfortunate situation, but you don't need to feel guilty about it. You have just done a painful thing, not a bad thing.

Parents use guilt to motivate children to fit into their mold of how children should be. Friends and lovers alike may try to use it. But just because it works on others doesn't mean it has to work on you. Guilt-givers use it as a tool to get what they want in a sneaky, covert way. When confronted by a guilt-giver, ask them in the most non-threatening, innocent fashion, "Are you trying to make me feel guilty?" This stuns them. It reveals their plan. They will probably deny your discovery. This is a very effective method for interrupting their usual guilt attacks.

A lot of people feel guilty about having fun because they feel they don't deserve it. They feel it's a bad thing to be sneaking away from their serious life to escape into a life of fun before returning to the "real world" to face the misery. That's crazy. You're not escaping into a fantasy world of fun; you're enjoying life the way it was meant to be enjoyed. Having fun will refresh you and help you face life's challenges. If you really need to be doing something other than your fun activity, skip the fun and do what needs to be done. But if you are just out having fun and have no reason to feel guilty–then don't. You deserve the joy.

Most of us can spot other people using guilt, but we fail to see how we manipulate ourselves with guilt. You feel guilty because you didn't do your taxes, pray to God, visit somebody or get your library books back on time. Turn your guilt feeling into a positive force. If you're feeling guilty because you haven't been exercising, get off your ass and go for a walk. Do your taxes, say a prayer, visit that friend and take the library book back. Ta da–no more guilt. If there's a way to take action against guilty feelings, then take it.

We're all going to make mistakes, but what if you were a doctor or a professional athlete? If you were to focus on the people who died or how many times you struck out or dropped the ball, you would be finished. You've just got to keep going and save who you can or get the touchdown when you can and forget about the balls that you dropped. Learn from your mistakes and hold your head high so you can remain a positive force in the world.

Once you become aware of guilt in your system, you will discover many attempts by others to encourage those feelings within you. We are bombarded with guilt to donate to the homeless, the hungry and dozens of other worthy causes. But if you're feeling guilty because of all the problems in the world, where is that going to get you? Yes, you may be very lucky and have a wonderful life, but this doesn't automatically qualify you for feeling like crap because other people don't have a life as good as yours. Be thankful for who you are and what you have.

When you're approached to give to a cause, never feel bad about not giving something you either don't have or don't want to give. Do the things you can do, do the things you want to do. If you want to give your money or support to those in need, do it with your heart and not your guilt. When you give with your heart, it will be a satisfying gift. When you give with guilt, it is just a way of dealing with your inability to tune out that flavor of Mind Poo. If you're a good person, living your life with compassion for others and reasonable morals, there is no reason for you to feel guilty.

Using guilt on people is not friendship and it's not love. Its sole purpose is to make them feel lousy. You can use love or affection or plain old communication. If you want people to behave a certain way, you just ask them for what you want in a kind, gentle manner. Whether you use it on others or let yourself be sucked in by someone else's guilt, it's a conscious choice you make. When people wrong you, ask them not to do it again. When you wrong people, then ask yourself not to do it again.

If you allow people to manipulate you with guilt, they will. It is impossible for you to be happy when you are passing on or receiving feelings of guilt. If you are actually guilty, then take responsibility and heal the situation. Be aware of fake guilt and get rid of it immediately. Don't be guilty about feeling guilty unless you are actually guilty.

A GUILT-RIDDEN SQUIRREL

Guilt is perhaps the most painful companion of death.
Coco Chanel

Tragedy

Smooth seas do not make skillful sailors. African proverb

You're wondering, what does tragedy have to do with having fun? Tragedy is never fun. It happens to everyone, though it may seem as if it happens to some more than others. It may be the loss of a job or a pet, a loved one, a relationship, or even a limb. If you were just about to retire, losing your life savings would be tragic. There are smaller tragedies like teenagers getting pimples on a first date, getting a date with a centerfold and being unable to perform. Passing up on opportunity for the wrong reasons. Tragedy is a natural part of life, and it can come to visit whenever it wants. If you can learn to take tragedy in stride, it will allow you to move past it and get on with your life. Right now, let's talk about death. I know death isn't fun, but let's have a look at this unpleasant chapter of life anyway.

Death is not only inevitable, it could happen at any moment. It can take weeks, years or even decades to get past the death of a loved one. But there is no right way to deal with tragedy and grief. There can be disbelief, rage, acceptance and grieving. Some people go through these emotions quickly, some never get past stage one. There is no specific time limit for grieving a loss. Grieving for an extended time doesn't necessarily show the depth of your love for that person. If you hold onto a state of monolithic misery, it will not benefit the person who has passed on in any way.

It is highly unlikely that a loved one would want you to feel despondent for years after their death. If you were to die, would you want all the people close to you to be sad? Wouldn't you want them to rejoice and remember all the wonderful times you had together? To relive those

Pain is inevitable, suffering is optional. M. Kathleen Casey memories in all their vividness and pleasure and then to move on to find someone else to enjoy life with is a beautiful way to deal with tragedy.

When tragedy strikes, it can challenge your deepest beliefs. Why did that tornado come to the trailer park and kill everyone? Why do good people seem to die for no reason? You will need to show courage to face a tragedy. If God is putting you through the ringer, it's probably because you're worth the laundry. When tragedy comes to visit, you'll need to figure out how to heal yourself. Maybe you need a leave of absence from work. Perhaps a visit to the site of the tragedy will help you close a difficult chapter in your life. Do you need to go on a spiritual journey to reach for something larger than yourself? If you're at the end of your rope, tie a knot in it and hang on; it's going to get better.

There is a natural healing process that will take its course. Healing from tragedy is not something that happens overnight, but having a good attitude will allow you to see your perplexing problems in a new light. Maybe this tragedy is just a test to strengthen you. By going through tragedy, you gain an incredible amount of courage and life experience. Take the time you need to heal, but make sure you set a goal so you know when to exit the tunnel of despair.

When I woke up on the morning of September 11, 2001 and saw those unforgettable images on CNN, I was stunned beyond belief. There it was, right there in front of my face on live television. Airplanes flying into the World Trade Center. Thousands of people dying because of some misinformed, Mind Poo-filled souls. An entire nation and a good part of the world was stunned in a heartbeat.

Though I didn't know anybody involved in this tragedy, I felt compassion for every single one of them. The lives they affected, the smiles they brought to people. I wondered if any of those souls had been waiting till later to enjoy their lives–to have fun, to live their dreams. It seemed so obvious that no matter where we are or what we do, our lives can be snuffed out without a moment's notice. Tragedy knows no boundaries and has no special victims. It was in that week of moments that I came to realize that nothing is permanent. I could die today and so could you.

It made a lot of people think about the fragility of their lives and how even though we live in a safe society, we are never truly safe. You have no idea when you or anybody you know will finish their earth visit. Out of that terrible tragedy have come some wonderful actions. New Yorkers pulled together like at no other time in history. People have donated millions and millions to help support the victims' families. There were many stories of amazing heroism, compassion or plain old human kindness. The 911 tragedy inspired many people to get out and live their lives.

Many people have had terrible things happen throughout their lifetime. You can chalk it up to bad luck or bad timing, but life isn't always fair. When darkness falls around you, start looking for the light switch. Maybe something good will come of it. Whether you slam your hand in the car door or you get your heart broken, pain lurks around every corner. That's life. If a tragic event in your life is holding you back from leading a happy life, dig into it and find out why. Feel the pain, anger, fear and sadness and then let those negative feelings go. Do whatever it takes to get happy and move on with your life.

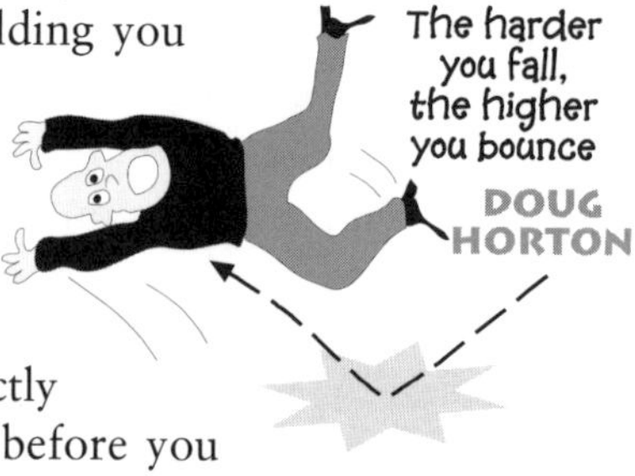

The seriousness of a situation is directly related to the amount of time that must pass before you can laugh at it. Look for the way to shorten the distance between the situation and when you can laugh at it. The tougher the times, the more we need to laugh and have fun to counteract them. There will be some tragedies like the World Trade Center attack that will never be considered something to laugh at. No amount of spiritual training, religious faith or positivity can prepare a person for the initial shock of a tragedy that large, but time heals and hopefully we can find something positive in our grief.

When it gets dark enough, you can see the stars. Lee Salk

Your tragedy may be less intense than death, but it is tragic all the same: a house fire, car accident, being the victim of a serious crime like rape, losing your job, breaking up with your sweetheart, a physically debilitating accident or serious illness. Tragedy happens to good people and bad people. Young or old, nobody is safe from its wrath. The best thing you can do is hold your head up high and count your blessings.

Death and tragedy remind us to focus on the things we need to be doing–like living, loving and laughing. Since you're going to die anyway, why not enjoy your life and the people in it before you do? Live your life before tragedy strikes. Trust that every bad situation will eventually work itself out. With the passage of time, it will be easier for you to see things more clearly. What does not destroy you will only make you a stronger individual. Regaining a fun attitude will stimulate your life and help you deal with your problems. If you can't laugh at your problems, you certainly can't put them in a sandwich and eat them.

Eat a live toad first thing in the morning and nothing worse will happen to you the rest of the day. Unknown

Mind Poo Wrap-up

May the forces of evil become confused on the way to your house. George Carlin

There are a few other flavors of Mind Poo, like control, perfection, jealousy, manipulation, rudeness, gossiping and revenge, which can be detrimental to your happiness. We have become so used to them in our daily lives that we begin to think of them as normal states.

Mind Poo can never be eliminated. It has the license to broadcast all over the planet. All you need to do is simply flip the tuner to a channel that is broadcasting a happier message. Of course, we all want to be free of suffering and negative emotions, but we need to be proactive in solving our problems and discovering solutions on every level. Sometimes there is a root to the problem, sometimes there isn't. The point is not to stick a fork in your back and keep rotating the fork and wondering why it's so painful; just take the fork out.

Admit you are having problems so you can get rid of them. Figure out what is tuning you into these negative radio stations. If you fail to deal with them, they will eventually convince you that you are worthless, that you are inadequate and undeserving of a giggle-filled pleasure ride in life.

Would the real you (I mean the you that keeps your heart pumping, your brain thinking and your muscles moving) want you to feel bad? Never. The sole purpose of the real you is to keep you at your optimum level of health. Getting past Mind Poo will allow you to hear your intuition and your heart. Following your heart will always take you to the right place. Trust the

Whoever gossips to you will gossip about you. Spanish proverb inner you. It knows a lot more than you give it credit for. When all the stress, anger, fear, sadness, guilt, jealousy and hang-ups are gone, all that's left is beautiful you.

Mind Poo is a natural part of life, but it's not you, it never has been you and it never will be you. You may get angry, sad or scared, but you are not those things. Mind Poo can be totally irrational but decline to be outfaced by irrational things. You are not a storage facility for negative emotions. Watch out for the trolls and dream-crushers. Every minute that you remain caught in Mind Poo is sixty seconds of lost happiness.

You have a choice: you can be an optimist or a pessimist. You can see the best of a situation or you can see the worst. True optimists will tell you that if you think positively everything will be OK, but you are still going to have negative experiences and feelings no matter how much positive thinking you do. Nevertheless, it's a lot easier facing life's troubles with hope and cheerfulness than it is when you're depressed and grouchy.

The pessimist sees difficulty in every opportunity. The optimist sees the opportunity in every difficulty. Winston Churchill

What I can't understand is why people will fight tooth and nail to stay miserable. They have so much opportunity to break free of the blues, but they just can't take the thought of letting go. Then they get together with other negative people and share all their Mind Poo to brew a batch of negative stew. Whether it is in business or in life, stay away from these people. Don't eat the stew at the Negativity Café.

Having a fun way of thinking is wonderful therapy for counteracting these negative states of mind. People who put their minds on a negative-thought fast do not become nincompoops who live in a make-believe world. They become happy, peaceful souls. Grab this problem by the horns–the real you is a sparkly spirit that wants to be happy.

I've never seen a monument erected to a pessimist. Paul Harvey

If you're currently carrying lots of baggage, it's not that you deserve it. It's the fact that you have chosen to keep it. Your body is not a cruise ship for vacationing negative thoughts. Confront your Mind Poo and courageously face your problems head on. Never deny your troubles but never own them either. Do you want all this Mind Poo around until you're dead? If you are full of Mind Poo, there will be no room left over for happiness or fun.

If you've spent a good part of your life being trapped in Mind Poo, don't expect to change in an instant. You have the knowledge and the tool of personal choice to get you out of it, but you will drift back. Mind Poo will work hard to try to prove these theories wrong, so why not try to prove them right? That way you are in control of making your life a pleasure-filled joyride rather than an uninspiring, day-to-day survival test.

You create your life with words if you use the words of Mind Poo; why not create a good life instead? Plow through the waves of Mind Poo, the antagonistic, non-supportive people–and notify the world that you are ready to hang out with some fun people. They will show up.

Maybe you need professional help with the Mind Poo you are experiencing. Maybe you just need a weekend of adventure. It could be as simple as taking the time to read a good book or go for a walk in the woods. Do whatever it takes. Until you be-come uncompromising in your extermination of extraneous Mind Poo, you will be destined to be miserable. Make stomping out Mind Poo an absolute priority.

If two wrongs don't make a right, try three. Source unknown

The Right Moment

Someday we'll look back on this moment and plow into a parked car. Evan Davis

Before you can have fun, there is one more unfun habit that has to be broken ... living in the wrong moment. Being out of the moment is when your mind is somewhere your body is not. Living in the "Now" is more than just a new-age voodoo ritual or something a guy named Buddha dreamed up 2,500 years ago; it is a fantastic way to live.

Let's start with the past. The past has passed–it's done, finito, over! All the anger, cussing and tears cannot change history. No matter how much time, effort and energy you spend on trying to alter it, the past is not open for change. Why climb into the boxing ring and get slapped around by events gone by? Living in the past just wastes fresh tears on old problems.

Some of us get stuck on the "Good Old Days Syndrome," where everything in the past was so much better. Gas was cheaper, people were more honest and the government wasn't so corrupt. Times change, so suck it up and deal with it. All you have is this moment–right now.

Then there are those of us who seem to live exclusively in the future. We postpone our pleasures and happiness, hoping for a better tomorrow.

But why leave your fun to some day in the future? Someday is not a day of the week. Will everything be OK when you finally buy a house? Then will you be happy? When you lose ten pounds? When you

get your new job or your new car? When you get a new hairdo? Then will your life be great? Why put off your happiness until a later date like Friday night or Sunday morning or this summer or next winter? When people retire, they begin to golf, travel and live life to the fullest. Why wait till retirement? That would be silly. Avoid placing your happiness in a future time zone, because if a piano hits you before you get to live your life, you are going to be really upset. Plan for a great future, but that's all you can do. Having fun is not the final song, it's the whole concert.

So you can't change the past and you can't predict the future. All you have is right now. To be here now gives you all kinds of benefits. Staying present helps you to enjoy and focus on the task at hand. Being in the moment will increase your work efforts, your capacity to communicate and, best of all, your ability to embrace life and love it.

Nostalgia is OK, but it's not what it used to be. Unknown

The more you can become aware of your now moments, the more fun you can have. I love whitewater rafting. When I'm in the front of the boat and the wind is blowing, the water is rushing beneath the rubber floor and there's a ten-foot wave coming my way, the very last thing on my mind is any kind of trivial worry. When that wave hits, all I am concerned about is enjoying the adrenaline and excitement of the ride. Enjoying life keeps me right in the middle of the moment.

The more fun activities and good times you partake in, the less the Mind Poo can sneak in. Mind Poo plays a big part in letting you regret the past and worry about the future. A great way to stay in the moment when the Mind Poo's chatting up a storm inside your head is to ask yourself out loud, "What does this have to do with right

now?" Just keep asking yourself that question until you say the answer is: "Nothing." Don't let Mind Poo destroy your moments.

There is nothing wrong with looking at the past, just don't dwell on it. The future is a celebration of possibilities, so thinking happy thoughts about it is encouraged. Enjoy everything you can, while you can. You never know when your life will end or your circumstances will change. Climb more mountains, take more trips, watch more sunsets, tell your friends that you love them, start that art class or go running up and down the street naked.

You can't let one bad moment spoil a bunch of good ones. Dale Earnhardt

Happiness cannot be traveled to, owned, earned, worn or consumed. There is only now, and if you're too busy living in the wrong moment, you may never get another chance. What if something tragic were to happen and you became dead? Could you leave here satisfied that you'd enjoyed your life? Play in life on every level and enjoy your life right now, today. You never know when it can be taken away from you.

It doesn't matter what your religious beliefs are, the Now moment is a magical place. Being in the moment somehow helps you to connect to your spiritual self. Spend a moment to feel the sun on your face, to smell the wind, to hear the birds and to see life unfold. We certainly want to be in the moment when driving down the road, so use that nowness whenever you can. Greet every moment with appreciation and delight right now. Being focused on the moment will expand your pleasure of it.

Be unrelenting and uncompromising in your pursuit of happiness. Get rid of the problems that take you out of the moment. If you're down at the beach and you're worried about getting your taxes done, then get home and do your taxes.

Don't try fooling yourself into having fun if you're ignoring chores that need to be taken care of. Take care of those Mind-Poo triggers and get living again.

One day you will no longer be here; one day you may no longer have your mobility. Now is the time to enjoy life because, yes, it could get better, but it could get a lot worse too. No matter how your life is, whether you perceive it as pleasurable or miserable, those feelings will not last forever. There will always be an assortment of experiences that can bring you happiness, sadness or both. The real fun in life is in the journey, to enjoy each and every moment. Appreciate that life is fragile and that there may never be a moment quite like this one. Never under any circumstances be happy tomorrow when you could be happy today.

I try to learn from the past, but I plan for the future by focusing exclusively on the present. That's where the fun is. Donald Trump

Sign Me Up For My Oneness with Funness

Life is either a daring adventure or nothing. Helen Keller

You know that anybody and everybody has the inbred capacity for fun. You know that it is plenty good for you in your physical, personal and professional life. You learned about how Mind Poo repels fun. You even know what moment to be living in. Gosh darn, we are doing fine. We went through all the cerebral crap and now it's time to make it happen.

So how exactly do you start? You need to make a solid commitment to yourself. Not "I'll get around to it someday, next year or when I retire." Everybody deserves to be happy and avoid suffering and so do you. Most humans will think long and hard about any commitment. How long will it take you to think about committing to a life of joy? A week, a day or just a few seconds? You need to commit this moment, this second, I mean right now.

Nothing ever stands still on this planet. All people, things and events are changing every moment–nothing remains the same. Change already happens in your life all the time anyway. You change your clothes, you change lanes on the road, you spend your change and the weather changes. You change from a baby to a child to a teenager to an adult. Your conditions change, your job changes, the people in your life change and nothing is ever the same. You never have to worry about change; it only happens one step at a time.

With a little perseverance, you can overcome your negative conditioning to make positive changes in your life. This will not happen overnight. You can't just read this book and la-de-da, the magic fairy comes by and sprinkles fun dust on you and you become the happy prince or princess. Every person is different, and you may find that it takes months or even years for significant change to take place. At first it may seem unnatural to pursue a life full of fun.

COMMIT NOW

I first learned about a fun life when I moved to Lake Louise in the Canadian Rockies. Lake Louise attracts people from all over the world. Australians, New Zealanders, Canadians, Americans and Europeans. Most of the adventurers who had come to this area believed that fun was something that could take place every minute of every day if you gave it half a chance. Before I arrived in Lake Louise, I had been surrounded by serious people who convinced me that fun was something you could have on weekends if you slaved your butt off all week. I had to put my preconceived notions aside and look at my life from a different perspective.

My life of fun started when I believed it to be possible. I knew I couldn't control my life and how it unfolds, but I could control how I felt about it. I used to think that life was supposed to be a struggle. I had no idea that you could have so much fun in a single day, never mind every day. I had to commit to never live like a programmed robot ever again. Once you commit to the possibility of enjoying every day, that is the beginning of your oneness with funness.

People are about as happy as they make their minds up to be
ABE LINCOLN

The more fun you have the easier it becomes. As you continue, it will become more natural and more important to you. So many of us have spent so many years avoiding fun that it takes some time to mentally understand and develop these concepts. But the longer you ingrain these ideas into your brain, the more genuine and long-lasting they'll be.

We become so habituated in our lives that we continue to do some actions not because they're beneficial but because they are familiar habits. All you need to do is make some new habits.

I can hear you saying, "Hey, I think my life is OK. I'm comfortable where I am, thank you." News flash–comfortable is boring!

For any human endeavor to become a reality out there, it must become a reality in here, in the eyes of the beholder. Once you've decided where you want to go, you need to imagine the way you want to be. It's something about your brain. If it's going to happen in reality, it has to happen in your imagination first. If you want to win at the Olympics, visualize the gold. If you want to lose weight, see yourself as skinny. If you want to have fun in life–see yourself laughing and giggling. The clearer you are on what you want and where you want to go, the easier it will be for you to get there.

Whatever you can do or dream you can, begin it. Boldness has genius, power and magic in it. Johann Wolfgang von Goethe

You can't just talk about it, you have to decide. You must commit. Once the mind decides, the body simply follows and obeys. It will take more than a few words and signing up to make it a reality. You must be determined to take action with enthusiasm! You can do amazing things with your life when you have your heart in it.

There is only one person on this planet who can make you happy and that's you. The government, material things or lovers cannot achieve what you can in a flash. A simple decision is all it takes. Decide to choose more fun, more often, wherever and whenever possible. Does a lifelong pursuit of bliss and happiness sound like such a bad idea? You can choose happiness or you can choose unhappiness. What's the absolute worst thing that could happen to you if you committed to a life of fun? You could laugh and smile yourself to your death!

The reason that fun gets put on the back burner is because nobody makes it a priority. Will you make fun a priority? How much more fun do you want in your life, ten percent or a hundred percent? The universe will give you whatever you ask for. All you have to do is get clear on what that is. If you don't know what you want, how do you ever expect to get it? When you firmly decide on something, it becomes a purchase order asking the universe to deliver it to you. The delivery date is determined by your desire for it to come true. Decide from this moment that you want more: more play, more fun, more friends, more good times. Hallelujah!

What would you pursue if you knew you could not fail? Do you want to skydive, get your pilot's license, learn to juggle, rappel off a cliff, go bungee jumping, sailing, golfing, check out caves, collect stamps, eat a grasshopper, jump from a boat, jump on a boat, join the mile-high club, ride a bicycle, swim with dolphins, swim with sharks, climb mountains, play the stock market, or eat strange food? Whatever pleases your mood is out there waiting for you. Make a goal to do one fun thing a day. If you did that for ten years, you would have accomplished 3,650 fun things.

Some sharks are mean and some are full of good times

Expect to gravitate towards what you think about most of the time. See yourself laughing and being happy. Develop a zest for fun, a glowing flame that can't be extinguished by anyone or anything. Understand that you can enjoy your life anytime, anywhere or anyhow just by believing it to be possible. You will never have a better life than you do already unless you desire it first. Maybe you have some Mind Poo that's saying, "Choosing to be happy all the time makes you a self-centered idiot." I would have to disagree. Choosing to be unhappy all the time is for self-centered idiots.

However, when you step out of the box of seriousness, your friends, relatives or co-workers may not support you and your appetite for joy. They may have difficulty wondering why anybody wouldn't want to be tormented like they are. The only way for them to deal with their boring lives is to knock down anyone within punching range. Take the advice of a giggler, not a grouch.

Catch on fire with enthusiasm and people will come for miles to watch you burn. John Westley

Deciding on a life of fun will quickly silence those anti-fun terrorists. Besides, once you are committed, who cares what they think? Is it more meaningful for you to be happy and proud, or miserable and accepted? Would you rather laugh or be right? Have fun or act important? Make it OK for giggles to wiggle their way into every corner of your existence. I understand you may be feeling challenged about taking on a fun attitude, but it's not that big a deal. How many smiles, days or years have you wasted already? Deciding to have fun is actually a decision to stop being miserable. If you're involved in some serious challenges, just lighten up and enjoy the battle. As long as you are alive, you still have a choice.

How are you ever going to have a fun life if you don't have some sort of guide or road map? There is a great sense of pride and satisfaction in achieving what is close to your heart. Humans are goal-striving machines–it seems preferable for us to have a target to head for. Take the time to figure out what your goals are. So many people never take the time to plan their lives out. They'll spend more time writing a grocery list than they will trying to determine their main goals in life.

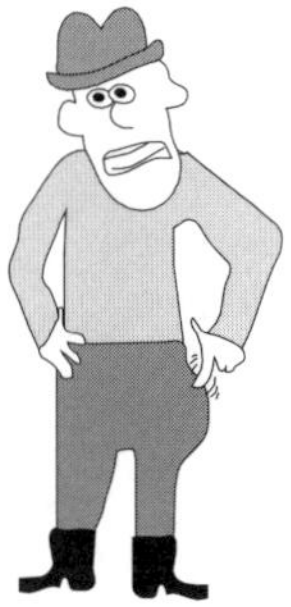

Instead of haphazardly wandering through life, fun people have a plan. Yes, not every plan works, but having a plan is better than no plan at all. If it doesn't work out, you can adjust your plan. Goals help you to see what is good for you and what is wasting your time. Be decisive and think carefully about what you want to do. You need to have goals, no matter how big or small. Whether they are close or far away, you need to have goals. Don't settle for less than you deserve.

I like villains because there's something so attractive about a committed person; they have a plan, an ideology, no matter how twisted. They're motivated.
Russell Crowe

Good goal-setting comes from good questions. What is it that would really make me happy? What lifestyle? What work? What kind of people do I want around me? What would make me feel good today? Would I like more fun and joy? How much? Can you imagine if everything in your life was chosen by you and not by what you thought other people would approve of? Sometimes we are less than honest about what we want because it may be socially unacceptable. If you have a dream, why aren't you pursuing it? Is it because you don't think you can or you don't think you should?

Determine the steps you need to take to get there, then start climbing the damn stairs. What is currently holding you back from achieving your goals? Are the goals in your life your goals or are you achieving them to please someone else? Are your goals unrealistic? Or do you just believe them to be? If you think they're impossible, you'll be right. Plan it out in stages. Don't get ahead of yourself and don't expect big changes immediately. You make your life happen, it is not something that just occurs. So much potential lies within you. Can you imagine all the positive ways you would be contributing to the planet just by becoming a fun person?

To have a happy life, you need to be constantly thinking about who you really are, what you want to do and where you want to go. Re-engineer your life so that all your dreams come true. Focus on the activities and people that you really enjoy. Then figure out what it will take to close the gap from where you are to where you want to go.

Regain control of your destiny. Your words have power and what you say will create your reality. Have the vision, feel the giggles and feel the love. Why not imagine a magnificent life? What harm is there in heading out for a wonderful destination? Solidify your attitude advantage. Choose to enjoy life no matter what happens. Being serious and miserable is not a natural way to live. There is a goal exercise at the back of this book, but do it after reading the rest of the F Word. Next, let's learn to appreciate what we already have.

You can wait forever for Mickey Mouse to come to your house or you can just go to Disneyland.

Attitude of Gratitude

If you can't be happy where you are, it's a cinch you can't be happy where you ain't. Charles "Tremendous" Jones

Happiness is not about having what you want, it's about wanting what you have. Whatever you have in your life is a gift and should be cherished. This concept is so simple that it's often overlooked. Count your blessings and be thankful. It begins with you appreciating the little things. The worst day being alive is still better than the best day being dead. The best gift that has ever been bestowed upon you is the gift of life. Are you breathing? Did you get to eat today? Did anybody let off any smart bombs in your neighborhood? Do you have electricity or toilets? What about a place to live? You can read, that's got to be worth something. People in developed countries have better lifestyles, more opportunities and more entertainment than ever before in history.

The richest person isn't the one with the most; it's the person who needs the least. We tend to focus on the one or two things that are wrong with our lives and completely disregard the hundreds of blessings we do have. When we get the things we yearn for we still want more. People have ten times the amount of stuff that they really need. How come they aren't ten times happier?

When we in the West compare ourselves to most of the planet, we are very lucky. Can you imagine living in Afghanistan under Taliban rule where there was no music, shaving was illegal and women were not allowed to learn, work, show their faces or leave the house unescorted? In our own slice of the world there are people starving, living on the street that are addicted to alcohol or drugs.

Even though we know that we have it so much more comfortable than most we still can't shut off that little voice of discontent. People come from all parts of the world and feel they are so lucky to live in such an abundant society. Why are we so oblivious to that attitude? We want everything to be better, but if you had everything then you would worry about where to put it all.

Do you think your life would be better if you were born rich? Or if you had more mental skills or athletic ability? Then would your life be better? People with more blessings than you aren't necessarily happier than you. Besides, you could be poorer, uglier and sadder than you already are.

Now, when it comes to your health, look at all the complex systems in your body: respiratory, circulatory, reproductive, muscular, nervous, cardiovascular, digestive, immune and lymphatic systems. Your ability to communicate: your vision, hearing, taste, touch and smell. The way your bones, muscles and joints work together to give you mobility. You are your own personal symphony of excellence.

Like when I'm in the bathroom looking at my toilet paper, I'm like, "Wow! That's toilet paper?" I don't know if we appreciate how much we have. Alicia Silverstone

The people who lead active and fulfilling lives are the earthlings rejoicing in what life has already given them. Look at your friends, your accomplishments and your travels. If this doesn't mean much to you, you aren't really giving your gratitude a chance. Why not focus on the rainbows instead of the downpours?

Is there something about your job that's good? Maybe you get some perks or flexible hours. Appreciate the people you work with. Enjoy the company of your cohorts and their sparkly qualities while you're together. Your job could be worse. What if you were a rectal thermometer tester (my apologies to all you testers out there)? What if you had no job at all?

Often we only appreciate things after they're gone. When I cycled around North America in 1993, what I appreciated the most were showers and home-cooked meals. Doesn't seem very exciting, but getting a shower after a week without one is a pretty exciting experience. These are the little things I'm talking about. Until they are taken away, we rarely if ever are thankful for what we have.

What if you were crippled in an accident? How much would you appreciate your mobility then? What if you lost someone close to you? Did you really appreciate him or her while they were here? Why wait for things to leave your life before you appreciate them? Nothing lasts forever–enjoy them while you can.

A HOMELESS PERSON

We find it easy to appreciate the beauty of the world when we go on vacation. Why only on vacation? You have sunrises and sunsets in your world too. Just because they are there every day doesn't make them less beautiful. The beauty of a foggy morning, the smell of fresh green grass. You can appreciate the benefits of where you live–there must be so many.

When you learn to appreciate nature, you have an unlimited supply of pleasure. No matter where you are in the world you can still enjoy a cool breeze across your face, the smell of the night air, the songbirds and the heavens. The diversity of the animal kingdom and the complex systems that work together to keep them alive are things to celebrate. There are sunsets, sun-rises, spectacular mountains, rolling plains, grand trees, aromatic flowers, infinite stars and galaxies, melodious birds, hopping frogs, fantastic fjords, violent volcanoes, deep blue oceans, feisty fish, colorful coral, stupendous storms and numerous other natural creations on the planet.

You can appreciate the diversity of our religious and cultural traditions. What about all the people who were involved in building your life? Your parents, teachers, coaches and mentors–all have something you can treasure. Be grateful for all the modern conveniences we have, like cars, telephones, computers, the Internet, TV, VCRs and other big-kid toys, the movies you can watch, the books you can read and the fun activities available to you in this day and age.

So wherever you are, no matter how much you have or don't have–just appreciate it. When you lower the bar a bit for what turns your crank, you'll be amazed at how damn enjoyable your life can be.

One of the things I truly appreciate is delivered food. Whether it's room service or pizza, all you have to do is pick up the phone, dial some numbers in a specific order, tell the person what you want and like magic they appear at your door a little while later. You give them some cash and they're on their way. Is that amazing or what?

Look at all the freedoms we have. When you go to the supermarket you can have almost any kind of fruit, vegetable or meat from all around the world. There are restaurants representing every kind of food there is. There is easy accessibility to beautiful art, music, architecture and diversity from every corner of this lovely blue planet. Just because you don't own something doesn't mean you can't appreciate it.

Value your life and all the dimensions of it. In other parts of the world, people have no SUVs, pizza delivery or health plans; all they have is famine and constant survival challenges. Imagine being homeless or begging for your next meal or eating out of a garbage can. You don't have to look to Africa to see how lucky you are. There are starving people right there in your own community.

If you lived on the street, there probably would be few opportunities for fun or laughs. But for you, look at how much opportunity there is for entertainment in your life compared to, let's say, your grandpa's. You can easily go sailing, mountain biking, see movies with sound and color, go to Disneyland or whatever it is that you do. Today you can travel easily with little infringement upon your budget. Fifty years ago going to Mexico was the adventure of a lifetime; now it's just something to do for a week in March.

If I had to build my own road system and pay for fire, police and ambulance service, it would certainly cost more than I pay in tax. The mail is a wonderful invention. For a few cents, I can send a letter around the world. I can do it for next to nothing since the invention of e-mail.

Men are slower to recognize blessings than evils. Livy

Do not put your attitude of gratitude on the schedule for next week because wherever you go, you may never be there again. The people you meet, the foods you eat and the sights and sounds you experience should be soaked up with the speed of the leading paper towel. You may never return, these people may die and the environment could change. Yes, that's a little harsh but it's absolutely true. When you remember the World Trade Center attacks, you realize that all those people vanished in a moment. Appreciate what you have because you just never know when lightning will strike you down.

Intensify your appreciation by celebrating. Sure, you probably celebrate the big things like birthdays, Christmas and the usual stuff, but there is more to celebrate than special events. Celebration is a part of human life. Celebrate however, whenever and whatever the heck you want. Celebrate that you woke up today and have another chance at happiness. Celebrate because you bought a new CD, or that you had some chocolate cake, you have a job, you don't have a job, the invention of toast, where you live and the success of your friends, good neighbors, spring, summer, rain, no rain, your pet, not having to make your own clothes, your plants, a really great dessert, a movie, good sex, a day off, or a chance to sleep in.

Celebrate the skills and talents you already have. Everybody is good at something–his or her special purpose. Praise yourself when you do something right. Take your rewards when you can. Don't celebrate when you get there, celebrate along the way.

Let us be grateful to people who make us happy; they are the charming gardeners who make our souls blossom. Marcel Proust

What if you knew that this would be your very last day on the planet; how would you look at the world? If you are going through tough times in your life, it may be a little difficult to get excited about things. You may have experienced tragedy close to you, but you can still celebrate. If someone has passed on, remember the good times you shared together. Give thanks for being allowed to participate in the game of life with this person. Yes, tragedy hurts and no one ever expects it to happen to them (that's why they call it tragic). Be sad, heal yourself and get back to celebrating life

There is no easier way to diffuse an overwhelming situation than to appreciate the little things. When things are getting really nasty, take whatever has you most upset and force yourself to find something good about it. A little bit of gratefulness will help you to melt away your upsets. As doors of happiness close behind you, new ones will open in front of you.

DON'T BE A GLOATING GOAT

When you do figure out how to appreciate what you have, don't bother going around announcing all your newfound pleasures. All those people that are a little worse off than you don't want to hear how much you love the clouds and the stars. People may start dry-heaving when you release your torrent of appreciation out into the public. If you are actively loving life, enjoy it with your inside voice. Sure you will slip up every now and then and blurt out some signal of gratuitous pleasure, but try to keep it to yourself. When you are buzzing through life, people will appreciate your happy energy more than your stories of appreciation.

Get excited about life and be an understated fun wizard. Celebrate wherever and whenever you can. Appreciate that life is fragile and you may never have a moment quite like this ever again. Enjoy your life like you would climb a mountain. Keep your eye on the summit but enjoy the sights, sounds and feelings on the way up. This concept of easy appreciation can totally change your life forever.

Do you realize what this means? The fact of being alive ... I still find it staggering that I am here at all. Christopher Leach

Expand Your Brain

If there are no stupid questions, then what kind of questions do stupid people ask? Do they get smart just in time to ask questions?
Scott Adams

If you could conquer most of your problems or at least handle them with more grace, humor and positivity, would that help you in your happiness quest? Of course it would. Somebody, somewhere on the planet, has experienced the challenges you are experiencing right now. They have spent years of their life understanding and documenting their troubles. Then they make this information available to you so you can deal with your problems a little more easily.

Learning is a matter of happiness survival. Learning stimulates your mind to think more, to be more. It opens up all kinds of opportunities, from friendships to careers. Gaining knowledge gives you increased confidence, boosts your value in the marketplace and expands your understanding of the world.

You can discover new physical activities that you never thought pos-sible. You can learn how to enhance your relationships, be a better parent or how to have that always evasive G-spot orgasm. What about compassion or patience or problem-solving skills? Maybe you just want to learn another language or how to fix the kitchen sink the next time it springs a leak. Learn how to recognize normal life changes–mid-life crisis, marital challenges, menopause–or read all you can about life-threatening illnesses like cancer or multiple sclerosis so you can take the best pos-sible care of yourself. Even a frightening experience like illness can be a voyage of discovery.

When you empower yourself with knowledge, you have an idea of what to expect and that's very comforting. Just as good warriors learn everything they can about the enemy before they make their move, nearly every problem can be improved, if not solved, with the proper skills and knowledge.

If you know more than your co-worker in your chosen profession, you will be worth more not only to your company but to other companies as well. If your company has to lay people off, do you want to be the least educated or the most educated when they have to decide who stays and who goes? If the industry you're working in is in dire straits, consider learning a backup career before they shut the mill. When the car came into existence, it didn't make much sense to keep building the horse and buggy, now did it? Just because you have a good career today doesn't mean it will be that way in ten years or even tomorrow. For every job lost in one field, another job is created in a different field.

Re-educating yourself for an entirely new career may not be easy, but it's a lot more fun than getting a pink slip from your job in a one-job town. If you're not updating your skills today, you will eventually become obsolete. Diversifying your knowledge portfolio gives you more options if something shifts. It's hard to have fun when your industry collapses. Learning how to survive under any economy or situation is just good foresight. I've worked in radio and television for many years and they just loved firing me. Not because I was a bad broadcaster but because I always seemed to be a wild card. Thank goodness I had photography skills that allowed me to buy a loaf of bread every once in a while.

We never get too fat and successful that we can stop learning.
Robert Redford

Knowledge, skills and understanding allow you to move more freely through life. Learning helps you discover who you really are and what is going on in the world. Your brain is like your physical body. If you stop using it, it shrivels and becomes useless. Don't see your lack of knowledge as a reason to feel shame, see it as an exciting opportunity. There's no need to be bogged down in the quicksand of ignorance.

As we grow up and move through the stages of life, many factors dissuade us from learning. Peer pressure, poor teachers, bad techniques, raging hormones. Maybe you failed a course and felt shame. Everybody has had at least one bad learning experience from their time in school. (Some of us had a lot more.)

Which teachers did you learn the most from? The ones you hated or the ones you loved? When I was in Grade 4, I tried out for the elementary school choir. The hellion lady on the piano said, "You are the worst singer I have ever heard." Do you think I ever sang again? Bad experiences or bad teachers can turn us off learning or ever trying again. The curriculum is set up to teach everybody the same way without any regard for different learning styles or personal motivation.

During my school years, a distaste grew in my mouth for learning because school seemed to be a jail sentence. Nobody took five seconds to explain to me why I was in school. I was told in no uncertain terms that I had to learn whatever they dished out. When I asked why we were studying calculus, I was told to shut up and sit down. Ten years after I left high school I realized that social studies would be handy if I traveled to faraway places. Or that English could teach me how to write my own book. Or that math taught people how to think logically. I saw the benefit of the information and I've had a love for learning ever since.

Where does this learning deterrent begin? A lot of people stop learning as soon as they finish high school or university. Do they know everything? They might think they do. Maybe you believe you can't teach an old dog new tricks. First of all, you are not an old dog and this isn't a trick. If you're out of work at fifty-three, who says you can't go back to university or technical college?

Do you believe education is too expensive? The average person spends hundreds of dollars on shampoo and haircuts in a year. Do you think it would be worth spending a little money on the inside of your head? How much is having a life full of options worth to you? Maybe you just don't have the time. After all, you have a hectic schedule. What's your excuse?

Curiosity killed the cat, but for a while I was a suspect. Stephen Wright

Part of the problem is that as we grow older, our childlike curiosity disappears. A child's desire to understand the world is fascinating. At that age we know we have the right to be curious about our world so that we can discover who we really are. As we grow older, we deny our natural curiosity, not only as a source of knowledge but entertainment as well.

Have you ever had the experience of living in a neighborhood for years and then notice a store or a restaurant that you never knew existed? Why does that happen? Because we forget to get curious about our world. There is so much that you can learn by observation. With your curiosity aroused and your awareness increased (here's where living in the moment really comes in handy), you will be amazed what you can learn in your regular day-to-day environment.

So maybe you had a bad experience or two. Maybe you haven't been paying attention. Maybe you haven't bothered to ask why. There's no reason to stop learning. You can never learn all there is to know and you can never learn too much. Your head will not swell up big and blow up from too much learning. You can't know everything, but you can certainly have a good time trying. Invest in your brain. It's important to keep your mind supple and to practice flexible thinking. Most humans are using less than ten percent of their brain. Imagine how much more room you have to store new experiences and new information.

There may be better ways of having fun and living life than you cur-rently know. Decide what you want to learn, decide what you have to do to make it happen and then get at it. The answer to almost every problem, challenge or situation is gained through knowledge and experience. You can do that through education, reflection, curiosity and awareness. You cannot grow and expand unless you're growing your knowledge. Be a master of your life, not a victim.

We are all born ignorant, but one must work hard to remain stupid.
Benjamin Franklin

So where can you learn? Get a library card. There are thousands and thousands of books that you are given access to just by getting that little card. Then there is the Internet. It seems like there is an informational-based website or a course on everything from fixing your car to building a birdhouse. You could take correspondence courses, begin an apprenticeship or read magazines. Go to college or university and take a day, night or weekend course. Open your eyes, your mind and your desire for more information. Once you begin to gain knowledge, you'll feel like a fish who finally makes it back into the water after flopping around on the beach getting scraped and frustrated. Knowledge is the clear water of life that will help you swim out of frustration.

Even if you aren't interested in getting a master's degree, the least you can do is learn from your mistakes. The only real failure in life is the person who never learns from their mistakes. Use every event, crisis and challenge to create a better life. Don't worry about screwing up . . . that's how you learn. If you open your eyes and ears and pay attention, you'll be impressed with what you can absorb. Learning is a skill that improves with practice. Learn from your mistakes and the mistakes of others.

Life is a constant schoolroom. Everything in your life happens for a reason. If you're having the same problems over and over again, you are not paying attention. Life will beat you down with the same lesson until you understand. Once you get the lesson, you can move on to the next stage. You can enjoy your days in the school of life and learn your lessons or you can skip class and learn nothing.

The more I traveled the more I realized that fear makes strangers of people who should be friends. Shirley Maclaine

Traveling is a wonderful way to learn about life. Thanks to all of our modern traveling machines, you can travel to anywhere on the planet with relative ease. Traveling offers you fascinating lessons about people, customs, food, art, entertainment and new perspectives to look at your life. Why would you not want to see the world? Are you scared, is it financial–what is holding you back? This earth is filled with so many wonderful people who live surrounded by astounding beauty. It's all there for you to enjoy.

Where do you want to go? Would you like to swim with dolphins in the surf off the coast of Australia? Ride camels by the pyramids? Drink wine and eat baguettes in Paris? Swim naked in a tropical lagoon? Or is hiking in the Rockies more your bag? This is the stuff dreams are made of. You have more opportunity to explore and discover this planet than at any other time in history.

Expand your horizons. It's not just about being happy where you already are–it's about discovering and adventuring to where you want to go. I dare you to see the world beyond your front door and what your television tells you. Until you leave your home, you can never discover what may be best for you. It could be new foods, new games and new methods of decorating your home. Discover art and music from faraway places. As great as we in North America believe our day-to-day life is, it is still a narrow view of the world. When you meet a person who has traveled extensively, they seem to be very balanced, compassionate, patient and inquisitive. Traveling is a source of pleasure and enlightenment. It lets you appreciate where you live and what you have.

The world is a book, and those who do not travel, read only one page. Saint Augustine

Education and fun are two words that belong together. Make learning a wonderful process laced with curiosity and adventure. You will grow as a person and as a spirit. Having fun while learning increases memory retention, and improves focus and concentration. The more fun you have learning, the more you will learn. Take away the stress and unrealistic expectations and you will groove on more knowledge. If you are not enjoying what you are attempting to learn, you probably won't gain knowledge very easily. Enjoy the process of learning, knowing that the absolute worst thing that could happen is that you become a wiser, more intelligent person.

The cure for boredom is curiosity. There is no cure for curiosity.
Ellen Parr

So, if you want more fun in your life, you have to learn about fun. Learn what makes you happy, what activities, what people. What way of living is most pleasurable to you? You could discover a little piece of information that could make sense of your life. Get to know fun the way you know how to walk and you will be one really happy person. If your mind is closed, you will never find those little jewels that can make your days better.

It is your ability to think that makes you who you are. There is so much that you may never understand, but learn what you can. Embrace learning as if it is a long-lost lover; love it, hug it and get aroused. Open up your mind, your eyes, your ears and your heart. Stimulate your brain and you will stimulate your life. Become a walking, talking, absorbing sponge.

Admitting what you don't know will be the beginning of your learning adventure. If you learn just a little every day, in five years from now you will be really smart. Ask yourself, "What could I learn today? How can I expand my possibility of having fun?" Learning is a treasure box waiting to be opened. Open it.

Everyone is born with genius, but most people only keep it a few minutes. Edgard Varese

You Were a Kid Once

It's never too late to have a happy childhood.
Claudia Black & Laurie Zagon

CHILDISH

Children perfectly exemplify how a fun way of thinking can bring you delight from the time you wake up till the time you go to bed. But acting like a child has a negative connotation in our world. We're supposed to grow up and stop acting like a child. There is a significant difference between acting childish and acting childlike. Childish usually means "immature, unreasonable or foolish." Childish behavior is temper tantrums, disobedience, impatience, pouting. It can be demanding, manipulative and attention-grabbing. This is why some animals eat their young.

Childlike qualities can be any or all of the following: accepting, adventurous, affectionate, alert, ambitious, artistic and amazed with the simplest of pleasures. Children can be caring, creative, curious, charming, cheerful, clever, courageous, expressive, energetic, enthusiastic, forgiving, free-spirited, friendly and funny. They can also be generous, gentle, glad, good-natured, honest, humorous and quick to forgive and forget distresses. These little adults are inventive and willing to learn mental, athletic, social and emotional skills every day. Children are lovable, open-minded, optimistic, outgoing, playful, spontaneous and totally involved in the moment. They find it easy to follow the language of the heart, to be trusting, uninhibited, nonjudgmental, unique, warm, witty and zany. These are the sparkly childlike qualities.

CHILDLIKE

Now, there was a time when you too were in awe of your world and free from worry. You had an attitude that allowed you to have your entire day smothered in amusement. You weren't concerned what the neighbors would think if you ran screaming naked through the sprinkler. Your imagination was not bound by the "realities" of day-to-day life.

The price of gas didn't dictate whether you were going to have a good day or a bad day. You didn't need the latest equipment to do an activity; you just made do with what you had. You understood that falling on gravel caused pain, but your skin would eventually grow back. You were excited to try new things and didn't care if you were good at them or not. Having fun was your main purpose in life. Fun was your only dimension.

When we were young, everything seemed possible, but as time went on the serpents of seriousness sucked us in. We began to do what we thought was right. We stopped acting childish but we also stopped being childlike. When you lump childlike and childish in the same category, then any childlike behavior may be looked down upon. For many of the serious humans, any kind of playfulness in the adult world is unacceptable. It's really quite sad when people fight back any glimmer of joy because of their perceptions about the "Right Way" to act.

You are only young once. How long that once lasts is the question.
Anonymous

Parents teach their children to walk and speak for the first two or three years and then they spend the next sixteen telling them to sit down and shut up. Adults become obsessed with making children into adults. They want to control them, pump them full of fear and motivate them through guilt. They tell them to be realistic and teach them to be careful, all in the service of being safe. Now, there's nothing wrong with being safe. The problem is that when you nurture someone with fear, they are probably going to turn out scared.

It's not just adults who wean children away from child-like qualities. Children themselves grow to an age when they want to break free of that "just a child" label. They no longer want to be associated with anything remotely considered child's play. This leads to further hardening of the child's attitudes. TV, peers and ignorant adults teach racism, judgment, neuroticism, snobbery and ridicule. Most kids are under pressure to be cool, to do well in school and for heaven's sake grow up.

Which part of being grown up should one look forward to? Would it be the stress, the seriousness, the sixty-hour workweek, wearing restrictive clothes, watching depressing news stories or judging the people of the world? Who made this rule about "growing up"? What is so wrong with having childlike qualities? If being mature is about being miserable, what's the point?

WHERE SERIOUSNESS BEGINS

You can only grow old when you stop laughing and playing. You may age physically, but you can always be young at heart. If you have lost your childlike qualities, would it be OK to reclaim some of them? What are some of the obstacles to play in your life? Who do you want to play with? Being childlike will overthrow those harmful or depressing thoughts and let you be free.

WHERE FUN BEGINS

Acting young exudes honesty and integrity. The best way to learn about children is to visit them in person. Baby-sit for friends or family or help out somewhere in your community. Maybe you even have your own. Pay attention to how they think, reason and operate. Imagine yourself thinking in those childlike ways. Let those beliefs saturate your consciousness. Find a baby to hold, and soak up all their warm, fuzzy feelings. You too can be naïve, new and innocent. Let the children in your life motivate you to be young again.

Being childlike is a state of mind, a state of mind that experiences joy at the drop of a hat. You can tap into that fountain of youth whenever you want to. What's wrong with having a glimpse of the world through children's eyes? It's time to deprogram that serious side of your belief patterns.

Make it OK for you to be childlike. Do whatever it takes to cherish the internal child that has been repressed for most of your adult life. Go to a toy store and buy some toys that bring you joy. Run naked through the sprinkler. Go ride a bike or roll in the leaves. Do whatever it takes to be lighthearted and fun. Be proud of your childlike characteristics and let them shine back into your life. Relax and be a kid again.

Beware of him who hates the laugh of a child. Johann Kaspar Lavater

Being Playful

We don't stop playing because we grow old;
we grow old because we stop playing.
George Bernard Shaw

Being playful is the true spirit of fun. In order to have a fun life, you need to be playful. There is no way around it. Everybody has a shade of playfulness within them, but just how often that comes to light is what determines your fun level. Every Master Fun Person I have met is gushing with a playful attitude towards life. You will rarely meet someone who is playful but not fun because the words serious and playful are rarely in the same sentence (except this one, of course).

A definition of being playful is the ability to take any given situation or group of items and be able to develop a game or a way of entertaining yourself with them. Being playful is willing to jump into activities without worrying if you look like a goofball. A playful person is quick to imagine and pretend to be something or someone other than themselves. Some words that come to mind are: merry, spirited, gentle, inquisitive, silly, boisterous, vivacious, jubilant and energetic. Add fearless of embarrassment; add a little flirtatious. Playful people love to surprise and be surprised. They are quick to laugh and love to horse around.

Playfulness is a way of participating in activities with joyful pleasure being the ultimate goal. Being playful is universal and instinctive to all of earth's creatures. Look at the way animals wrestle, bite, scratch, tumble, run and roll around; animals know that the ultimate part of life is to enjoy it. Play is an adventurous, challenging, stress-free, spontaneous activity that does not include a bunch of rules or winners and losers. Nor does it include tension, serious competition, hard feelings or criticism. There is a tenderness to play that cannot be forced out of anybody.

Being playful helps your imagination let go. It decreases stress; tests your memory; promotes abstract thinking; teaches patience, problem-solving and cooperation; sparks your curiosity; boosts your self-confidence; builds friendships and elevates your sense of humor. Play can help you develop speed, agility and balance. It fosters great team and sportsmanship skills. Playing can help you to discover the best of times and provide a remarkable connection to the people you are with. Being lighthearted accesses your natural ability to laugh and fights off Mind Poo in the process. It can also be a form of escapism from the daily grind of life. It will have you glowing with optimism instead of being suffocated by pessimism. It will improve your relationships and it will improve your day.

There is a difference between playing competitive games and playing hide and seek. Playing to win as opposed to playing to enjoy. Being playful is capturing that childhood energy and simplicity and putting it into your activities. If you say that you already play golf and tennis, you are missing the point. Playing and being playful are two completely different concepts.

As I grew up I was constantly reminded to act my age and not my shoe size. My peers made it quite clear to me that being playful was not cool and if I wanted to fit in I should grow up. Did you grow out of being playful and childlike or get talked out of it? We have convinced ourselves that play is immature and unimportant. When you were young, it was the process of play that helped you to understand the world. It gave you a chance to explore your surroundings, learn how they worked and how to relate to them. Along the way, we lose touch with our natural ability to think and act in a playful manner. As adults, the only games we usually play are mind games.

If life doesn't offer a game worth playing, then invent a new one.
Anthony J. D'Angelo

The problem is that we give a lot of weight to what people think about us. On any given day on any given street, there is somebody who is looking down upon being playful. Inside they wish they could recapture some of their youth by becoming playful themselves, but they don't and they don't want anybody else to either. The way they deal with their lack of playfulness is to ridicule or dissuade the people who are. They just aren't impressed with a bunch of yahoos yahooing it up.

If we listen to these naysayers, it's no wonder we stop "goofing around." Who cares what "they" think–it's what you think that matters. As individuals, it is oh-so-important to take ownership of what we feel like doing instead of what we think will be "cool" with everyone around us. When we shut down our playfulness to please others, we have given away our power to an already unhappy person. Why would we do that?

So moving past what other people think, we will need to evaluate how we play in life. Do you jump in feet first for the games at the backyard barbecue or do you watch everyone else from the sidelines? Do you play fair? Is your goal to have fun or to win? Do you only become playful when you are drunk or on vacation? When you participate fully in a playful moment, you become so lost in the situation you may actually connect to your spiritual self. Adults lose a wonderful gift of life when they grow up and become serious. Play inspires folks to remember the joyful side of being alive.

A FORM OF CATCH

I believe that everybody knows how to be playful in some context. It's whether or not the spirit of play is welcome to frolic with your personality. Could you add a playful attitude to some areas of your life? Like at the office or around the house? Instead of getting old and historic, why not consider becoming young and euphoric? Give yourself permission to play, then get out there and begin right away.

Every time I see an adult on a bicycle, I no longer despair for the future of the human race. H. G. Wells

You deserve to play every day if you so desire. You may have commitments like family, work, community service or religion that distract you from your playtime. But play and work do not have to be separate. You can take your playful spirit with you to all of these commitments and just make life a hugely enjoyable event.

Humanity has advanced not because it has been sober, responsible and cautious, but because it has been playful, rebellious and immature.
Tom Robbins

Set up a putting golf course through your office and play a game at coffee break. Crush up paper into balls and use the recycle basket as a hoop. Go to a toy store and buy some toys that you can bring to work. Buy action figures of your favorite cartoon characters and put them on your desk.

Our society generally believes that if someone is playful, they can't be taken seriously. There is some truth to that. There's a time and a place for play and it's up to you to read the situation and see if it's appropriate. If you have to make a presentation to a client, it may not be the best idea to do it with a clown nose and a tutu. On the other hand, if there's a theme party and you show up without a costume, you may be perceived as a fuddy-duddy. Learn to read the situation and test the waters before you jump in with the tutu on. Sometimes your playful attitude will fall upon deaf ears. Save it for another time.

When the opportunity arises for a playful moment, don't dilly-dally, jump in and give it your best effort. Don't be afraid of looking stupid; be more afraid of looking serious and stiff. Give yourself the permission because dammit this is your life and you deserve to enjoy it. When you get the urge to play it is a reminder from your spirit that you are not here to bust your ass every single day. Whenever you go to play at any activity, do it with your heart, do the best you can and enjoy every moment of it. Playfulness is gentle, innocent pleasure; it's yours for the taking.

Ignore the stereotype about what age should be doing what activity, whether it is tag, tobogganing, horseback riding, naughty dancing, lawn bowling or Scrabble. Do not let the recommended age on the box dissuade you from at least giving it a try. All the fun people I have ever met, regardless of whether they were fifty, sixty or seventy, considered themselves a boy or girl who is still young at heart.

Now, it is always more fun to play with others than it is to play with yourself (I have to ask myself if this is the best choice of words). Once you happy yourselves up, you will naturally want to get people involved so that you have someone to play with. Now just a word of caution about your newfound enthusiasm. This happened to me and it nearly knocked my socks off.

Some people don't like to sing

I met a really great fitness instructor at the community center. We began to talk about cycling and how much he loved it. I love to cycle too and I thought it would be great for us to go out for a ride. I kept pressing him to go for a ride, go for a ride, and finally with some sorrow in his voice he told me why he couldn't. Late one evening while out on his bike he was attacked by a group of men with bats. He was beaten senseless and left for dead. He hasn't cycled since.

If your potential playmate has had a traumatic experience in relation to your activity, it could just bring back a flood of awful memories. Never force a person to take part in an activity; you just never know why somebody doesn't want to play. Playfulness is gentle, and when people shy away from a playful activity just let it be. Inspire people to play when you can and just move on if they do not want to play with you.

Be quick to tell people when you have made a silly or foolish mistake so that you can laugh together.

The other key aspect of playing is that you do it fairly. Do it in the spirit of good sportsmanship. When you lie or deceive while you play, you betray the people around you and yourself. You are not trying to play, you are trying to win. It sends the message out that you can only do well when you cheat. Is this how you want to be perceived–as a cheater?

The odd time or two parents involved with community sports have been known to scream or lose their cool on the sidelines. They get into verbal spars with the parents in the stands. In a couple of extreme cases, people have died in fights that have broken out in the stands. What kind of message does this send out to your children and the rest of the children in the community? If you can't play right, go home and put a pickle in your bum.

Play fair, play games, play sports, play with new ideas. You can go to the park and chase a dog, roll down a hill or make up fantasy names for yourself and your friends. Be first on the dance floor when the opportunity arises. Go to the playground and jump on the monkey bars. Tickle your friend while standing in line at the bank. Spend an hour making a sign when you go to pick up a friend at the airport. Make tough-looking gingerbread men. Create a phone message that will make people laugh out loud. Jump on the bed in your hotel room on your next vacation. Sing crazy songs, have a good old-fashioned water fight with the hose or just play dress-up. Imitate your friends and family in a gentle but fun manner. Go to an art supply store and pick up what you need to do some drawing or painting. Shop at the dollar store for all kinds of cheap entertainment. Write stories or poems. If none of these work, go back to basics and go wrestle someone you love.

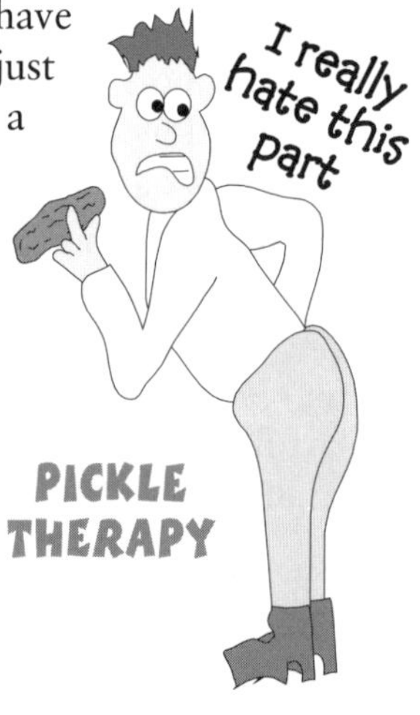

Take your childhood experiences with play and throw them into your adulthood. Live and work but never forget to play and have fun. Rediscover your playfulness, be playful and play on, my children, play on.

You can discover more about a person in an hour of play than in a year of conversation. Plato

Creativity

I can always be distracted by love,
but eventually I get horny for my creativity.
Gilda Radner

If you are a fun person, chances are you are quite a creative specimen. If you are creative, you probably have a good degree of fun to your personality. Creativity is the ability to generate new ideas and ways of looking at problems or challenges. Being creative can also mean being resourceful, imaginative, inventive, ingenious, innovative and unique. It means breaking rules and making mistakes. Some people think creativity is something that comes from outside their bodies. When it's flowing, it's like you are merely channeling the information as it comes down the pipes from heaven.

Now, you might be saying that you aren't very creative. That creativity is for the artistic community. You know, artists, musicians and architects. Well, that's just not true. Society may assign the job of creation to the so-called "artists," but everybody is creative to some degree. Single parents use their creativity to make ends meet, politicians create the illusion of leadership, accountants are creative with numbers and engineers are creative with their concepts of physics. Everyone is creative.

Yes, you may not be very good with a paintbrush or writing hit songs, but there's something in your life that you're very creative with. Any time you solve a problem, you are reaching the highest peak of creativity. Creativity lets you look for better ways to live your life.

Creativity begins with a problem that needs solving or an artistic vision that needs to be released. Adversity will motivate creativity. If you are experiencing a potential disaster in your life, your mind will work at lightning speed to create ways of getting out of it. Desire for money is a fantastic stimulation for creativity. If you're short on rent money, you will probably come up with a solution to avoid living on the street. Whatever it is that you desire, if you want it badly enough, your brain will work overtime to create a plan for how to get it.

Dreams and goals help you to be creative. They give you a target to aim for; then you have to figure out how to get there. Problems stimulate creative solutions, but so will love. When there is a potential for love, the heart opens up and inspires the brain. You may create poems, make gifts or bake a cake, whatever it takes to win the heart of your sweetheart.

In business, smaller companies win out over big companies in contract bids using their creative minds as their only tool. Creative advertising can make the difference between a company being successful or bankrupt. A creative mind helps to even the playing field. How do you start this so-called "creativity"?

A hunch is creativity trying to tell you something. Frank Capra

The more you challenge your creative instincts, the more powerful your brain becomes. The more exercise you give your brain, the more neural connections it will make. Create good times by avoiding routine in your life. Craft new ways to play, love, cook, work, socialize, live, eat, exercise, whatever. Commute a different way to the office; wear a different style of clothes; get up half an hour early for no reason. There are books, courses and people that can teach you how to be creative. When you express your creativity, you reveal the most wonderful parts of your being.

You can use your voice, your mind or your body in a creative way. Your tools may be a guitar, a kitchen, a workshop or your hands. You can sculpt, carve, paint, sketch or whatever you please. Figure out how to release your creativity and be proud of your creativity. Each creative endeavor you undertake will expand your creative abilities in all parts of your life.

If you look around, you can see creative inspiration everywhere. When you can see ingenuity in others, you can have more yourself. Take a car, for example. What a fantastic creation. Admire creative clothes, advertising, mall displays, parenting and architecture. Go to the local art gallery and have a high regard for the creative spirit of the artists on display. Enjoy the skills of bridge-builders, musicians, moviemakers and homemakers. You can be anywhere on the planet and appreciate the creativity around you. Just because you don't own the bridge doesn't mean you can't enjoy it. Whether it is God's creation of the earth or the creations of humankind, enjoy them all.

Every single thing that has been created by humans has begun inside somebody's imagination. Spark your imagination and discover more of life's jollies. Your imagination can take you on journeys of unfathomable proportions. It is one of the few things in the whole world you have absolute control over. You can go anywhere, be with anybody or do anything for free (no tax either). At any time of the day or night, you can discover a wonderful part of non-reality.

Never lose in your imagination. Never. Never. Never. Winston Churchill

How much do you use your imagination? How much could you use your imagination? Imagine in your head what a wonderful life you could create, then begin. Use your imagination to visualize where you want to go. You have a fairytale factory right inside your head. Great lives start with great dreams.

There is a difference between dreams and fantasies. Dreams are something you yearn for and you somehow believe them to be possible. Dreams are where you want to go and fantasies are an entertaining trip into the world of imagination. Fantasies are a vision that will probably exist only in your head. When we think of a fantasy, it is usually sexual. When people act out their fantasies, it can be fantastic or it can be detrimental. If you have fantasies about "doing" the milkman, it might go over well with the milkman but not your spouse. But if you experience that fantasy in your head and nobody gets hurt–what's the big deal? As a kid you probably played cops and robbers. Just because you pretended to be a robber, it didn't officially make you one. Just because you have a dirty thought or two, it doesn't make you a bad person.

A healthy imagination is a great happiness catalyst. If you're stuck, enjoy the imaginations of others. Like children or children's television. Movie companies like Disney are the mark of hundreds of minds coming together to create fantasy worlds. My favorite source of imagination inspiration is the *Weekly World News*, a supermarket tabloid published in Boca Raton, Florida: "Grandpa Trades His Wife for a Ride in a Space Ship," "Dog That Talks and Does the Dishes Too." I certainly would like to get me one of those dogs. Do these magazines have any credibility? They certainly do, in the imagination department.

DONNA THE DISH DOG

There are plenty of reasons to expand your imagination and plenty of inspirational sources around you. If there aren't, go find some. Your imagination may be sparked in times of reflection, while walking, driving or when you're in the shower. Do not edit your ideas, just go with your imagination and see where it takes you. Being playful encourages you to come up with your most creative ideas. Exercise your imagination the way you exercise your body.

Often, the only time people use their imaginations is to create the dreaded "Worst Case Scenario." All we can think of is what could go wrong. Actions and emotions follow thought, so you are actually moving the worst-case scenario into reality. Why rehearse for the worst when you could be imagining the "Best Case Scenario" instead?

TOM THE TIGHTROPE GUY

You have tons of potential to encourage your creativity and solve your problems faster. You have that ability within you, so if you don't like your options create new ones. You create your life, so why not create magic and delightfulness? You can imagine your way to happiness. Step outside the box in your thinking. Stretch your limits. Your imagination will lead you to wherever you want to go. Create, live, love and laugh!

Don't be so open minded that you brains fall out. Unknown

Say Yes

Action may not always bring happiness;
but there is no happiness without action.
Benjamin Disraeli

Any fun activity that you pursue begins with the word yes, but most of the time our tendency is to say no. We say no to strangers, beggars, salespeople or phone solicitors. We're constantly bombarded with requests to volunteer our time, give our money to a carpet cleaning company or join a spiritual movement. If we said yes to everything, we would have dual citizenship at the church while living at the poorhouse with no time to ourselves. It is totally understandable that we refuse most if not all of these requests, but there's a major side effect to this habit of saying no. You may miss a good opportunity and end up regretting it for your whole life.

Why do we say no to so many things? The training begins when we are tiny little babies. Get your fingers out of there, don't touch that, bad girl, bad boy, or the old favorite–why are you being so childish? Often our parents discouraged us from discovering what was around us because they didn't want us to get hurt. Or they simply didn't have the patience. At school we were consistently programmed to do and think as the teachers said. Peers may have ridiculed us for being different. If you were repetitively scolded for trying new things or questioning authority, it's no wonder you stopped venturing out of your safe little world.

Once we become adults, we are bombarded by requests for our money, our time and our energy. Often by our children. The cycle continues.

And religion and society teach that if we say yes to ourselves too much, we're being selfish. But people deserve to feel good, and saying yes helps to

let fun in. Just saying the word "yes" begins the process. Compare it to saying the word "no." Say no out loud with some passion. How did it feel? Light and fluffy or kind of intense? Now say yes. Say it with a smile. Say it out loud. Clap your hands while you say it. How did that feel? Felt great, right? Yes wins every time. Yes, yes, yes.

Saying no is like letting a little air out of the tires on your car. Whether you say it yourself or you hear it from someone else, no certainly isn't inspirational. When we want something in life, whether it be a date, a sandwich off the menu or a ticket to a concert, who likes to hear the word no? So often we say no when we could be saying yes. Every time an opportunity comes your way, it's just the universe's way of saying, "I like you. I would like to make your life a little more interesting. Please check this out."

It is better to live one day as a lion than a hundred years as a sheep.
Italian proverb

Dare to go a whole day without saying no. Do you think you can do it? Did you say yes or no? When you shut out new opportunities, life becomes routine. Maybe your fear convinced you that you were better sticking with what you know. There are plenty of fears–fear of the unknown, fear of looking stupid, fear of injury or just fear of new things. The positive effects of saying yes far outweigh the fears you may have. You may experience a little fear, a little discomfort, even a little lack of confidence. But none of those things will kill you. Perhaps you're afraid of becoming a happier person because you don't believe you deserve happiness. If that's the case, you need to examine that belief. Everyone is worthy of happiness because our essential nature is goodness.

Unfortunately, our world has some negative, repressed people who don't know they are fully deserving of happiness and so don't step outside their comfort zone. But you don't have to be one of them. It can be tough to say yes. Saying yes puts you into uncharted territory. Saying yes to fun is saying no to misery.

Maybe you don't have the skills or the proper knowledge to say yes to an activity. Then go out there and get them. Take a class that teaches you to snowboard or mountain bike or rock climb. Read up on the subject and maybe you'll find out that it's not as hard as it seems.

There could have been a traumatic event in your life that has been deterring you from leaving your comfort zone. Maybe you are naturally scared of new things. That's OK. Just start slowly and build on every little victory. If your fear is so debilitating that you have chained yourself to the house for safety reasons, get on the phone and get some professional help.

Maybe you're just lazy. It's not fear or lack of knowledge, it's not past trauma, it's just plain old laziness. We are naturally active creatures, but when we discover television, some of us never leave the couch. I don't want to knock anybody, but if you're saying yes to pizza, oversleeping and a pooch on your belly, you're saying "yes," but it's the evil yes of laziness. Step out of your comfortable, familiar world. When you stop risking, you stop growing. Safe choices lead to boring lives. If your life is too safe, maybe it's time to start risking.

You may attempt new activities that may not be successful, but that doesn't make you a failure. There are no failures. Someone who's willing to try without being worried about failure is a strong individual. If they do fail, they brush themselves off and get going again. You might fall on your face or be laughed at, but big hairy deal. Be proud that you're courageous enough to get off the couch and do something interesting with your days. When opportunity knocks, make sure you're there to answer the door.

Jump into the middle of things, get your hands dirty,
fall flat on your face, and then reach for the stars.
Joan L. Curcio

The person who laughs at you is just some lame soul with a boring life. Adventurous, fun people never laugh at people trying new activities. They were there once themselves, and when they see a brave soul like you get up there and try something new, it gives them the inspiration to continue and expand their own lives.

What is the worst thing that could happen? You find out that a certain activity is really not for you. Or maybe you discover something that you love but have been denying all your life. Every single time you say yes it gains momentum and gives you confidence. If it doesn't work out, at least you tried. Say yes to crazy ideas and dreams; say yes to things that make you feel good, like a rewarding career, physical, mental and emotional pleasures. Say yes to play and fun and healthy living. Say yes to the opportunities in front of you, but most important say yes to your life.

Try everything once except incest and folk dancing. Sir Thomas Beecham

You will be amazed how fun and entertainment will slide into your life. Every kind of activity has a fascinating subculture of folks who flock to it.

Whether it is rock climbers, mountain bikers, lawn bowlers, model train collectors, birdwatchers or sailors, each one of these groups has a wide range of individuals who come together for a common goal. When you become involved in new activities, you also have the chance to meet some of the most interesting people on the planet.

So many times I've met new friends, lovers or business contacts while out in the world sampling its delicacies. You just never know what will pop up in your face when you're saying yes to yourself and to life. Until you begin saying yes you will never know. Touch, smell, feel, see and experience the world.

Not only do you personally gain in your life when you say yes, but you inspire all the people around you to at least think about new possibilities in their own lives. They might not climb Everest just because you did, but they might buy a fitness membership and start to work out. Or go on that vacation they've always dreamed about. If we want to encourage our children to try new things, whether it's piano playing, football or hockey, don't you think we should be setting the example for them?

Opportunity dances with those who are already on the dance floor.
H. Jackson Brown Jr.

Maybe you've been saying yes to activities to impress others. Why not do things to impress you? Filter through all the restrictions that your relatives, friends or society have placed upon you. Actively cultivate the activities you want to do. If you're having trouble getting started, look for inspiration from photos or talk to others who have done what it is you want to do. Say yes to your dreams and your desires and most important say yes to you. Break free of the flock and the monotonous daily existence. There are infinite possibilities in little beginnings.

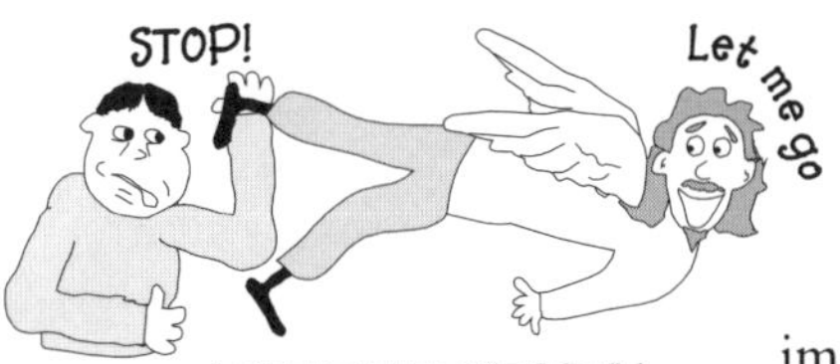

DON'T LET SERIOUS PEOPLE HOLD YOU BACK

Dare to say yes and begin saying it today. If you never say anything and you never do anything, you can be sure you'll never amount to anything. Saying yes changes your external world into a more delightful place. If you're willing to try new things in your personal life, you're more likely to try new things in your professional life and vice versa. There is an infinite amount of fun to be had. Say yes a few times and it becomes a habit. Saying yes consistently creates a fun-filled reality. Mmm, I like fun-filled reality … how about you? If there's only one thing you get out of this book, this is it. Say yes!

LEGS MCGINN

I believe in getting into hot water; it keeps you clean.
G. K. Chesterton

Spontaneity

One must not lose desires. They are mighty stimulants to creativeness, to love and to long life. Alexander A. Bogomoletz

Spontaneity–something caused by natural impulse or desire. Terms like spur of the moment or following your intuition come to my mind. Spontaneity gets rid of structure and control. It is the true essence of fun, a place to experience freedom. This is another wonderful childlike quality that seems to disappear as we go forward into adulthood. Spontaneity is not something you plan, it just happens. Something inside of you takes you in a totally different direction. Spontaneity brings fun, creativity, surprise and freshness to your life. Spontaneous states are usually short, eventful and full of inspiration. They seem to unfold naturally and give you a magical feeling of synchronicity, as if whatever has happened was supposed to happen.

Imagine your life being planned until the day you die. You go to work at the same time, take the same route to the office, eat the same foods and do the same things every weekend. No need to worry about the future because it will be exactly the same as today, except you will be older and you will have more polyester outfits.

Of course, you don't want your life to be exactly the same every day because then it would be boring. Variety is the life of spice and spontaneity will take you there. Spontaneity is listening to that little spirit within you that knows what fun is all about. Everyone has these natural urges, it's just a matter of whether you follow through with them or not. Fun people find it normal to be unstructured and live life as it comes.

Spur-of-the-moment thinking makes room for anything to happen and allows you to embrace it when it does. All you planners out there are probably cringing at the thought of no plans. It is extremely important to plan, but somewhere in

your plan you need to allow for spontaneous diversions. Plans are great until one factor changes: like the weather or you forgot something at home or your car breaks down or the amusement park is closed. So what. How often is happiness destroyed by overpreparation? Overplanning is the knife in the back of spontaneity.

Having a mind that is open to spontaneous thinking will trigger numerous opportunities for little joy rushes. Intuitively you know what makes you happy. Your intuition will guide you to exactly where you need to go, but if your thinking is clouded with Mind Poo, it may be very difficult to hear these intuitive messages.

Serious people seem to think that spontaneous conduct is a bad thing. If you partake in unstructured behavior, you may get yourself into trouble. Like unwanted tattoos, body piercing, credit card debt and even pregnancies (sexual desire has been known to trigger the odd spontaneous response). We all have millions of spontaneous urges, and thank God we have a filter inside our brain. It is called common sense.

Common sense is not so common. Voltaire

Common sense will tell us that we can't buy a brand-new sport utility vehicle just because we have an urge to. If everyone followed every impulse they had, there would a huge population explosion and anarchy everywhere. Now, acting impulsively is a wonderful thing. It sprinkles your life with var- iety and activity. But it can also be a quick way to gather up a lot of debt. Some spontaneous urges are good and some have a price.

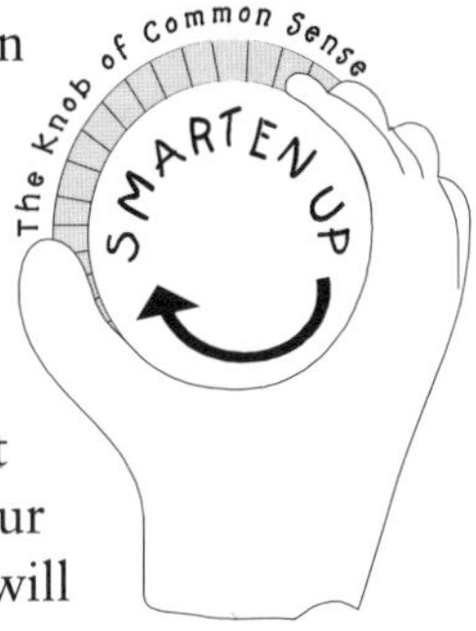

If, for instance, you have a spontaneous urge to run naked and prance it might be a problem if you are in customs at O'Hare Airport. If you see someone with a great body and you throw yourself upon them in a thrust of passion, you may seriously offend them. Common sense will tell you that there is a time and a place for spontaneity. Certain environments, people or situations just do not warrant spontaneous behavior. All the trials and errors of your life form your version of common sense, and hopefully it will guide you when you need it.

If your common-sense filter has been set to its highest setting, it will separate out most, if not all, impulsive urges. If you want more excitement and personal satisfaction, adjust the knob and let your spontaneity out for a run more often. Trust your common sense when confronted with an opportunity to step outside the box. Your common sense will stop you from overindulging in spontaneity.

So where does it all begin? Change your regular procedure. You could be a spontaneous eater. If you always eat Chinese, try Ethiopian. Go to a restaurant and pick the third entree no matter what it is. If you always go to western movies, go see science fiction flicks. Take your dog for a walk at three a.m. or sit on the edge of your roof to watch the sunset. Eat your dinner naked to the sounds of opera. Wake up in the morning to James Brown's "I Feel Good." Choose a movie by which one has the most letters or the fewest letters in the title. Beautiful things come from spontaneous actions. New ideas, solutions, activities, laughs and exploration can all be a part of it.

If you're an over enthusiastic planner, maybe it's time to loosen the schedule. Passionate plotting may create more anguish than it is attempting to solve. Can you find some time for a spontaneous diversion? Sure it makes sense to plan to be at the airport before the plane leaves, but if you're always on a tight schedule and your car blows a gasket, there's a good chance you will too.

What about your itinerary for a vacation? Are you the kind of traveler who tries to cram in as much activity as you can? What happens if you're on holiday and a rich man invites you to live on his yacht for a week to eat peeled grapes and watch exotic belly dancers? You say, "I would really like to but we've planned to see the museum of wool and, well, we bought the tickets six months ago." Dedication to the plan instead of dedication to fun will uncover more disappointment than you had planned for.

Fun people have no problems changing their itinerary on the spot. They take the best opportunity available regardless of their plans. They fully understand that you live life once and when they need to make a major turn in their course, they do it without regret and without hesitation. The universe is unfolding as planned–the challenge is that it may not fit in with your plans. So plan where you can and flex when you need to.

There is a difference between being spontaneous and canceling plans at the last minute. If you have made a commitment with someone, you should stick to it. But there are exceptions. My friend Luke has no problem making the best choice for him and I respect that. If we make a plan to go for a coffee and he gets an offer to go skiing free for the day–who am I to shut him down because of "the plan"?

If you truly love the people around you, don't you think it's important that they do what is most important to them and not what your appointment book says? In business, however, if you cancel your appointments because you have a better offer, it won't be long before you're out of work or out of business. Let your common sense guide you. If your friends cancel on you because something more exciting has come up, wish them well. If you need to cancel, make sure you're not hurting somebody's feelings before you run off. If you don't, you may have a great spontaneous adventure, but you won't have any friends when you get back.

There is a time and place for planning. If you're building a bridge, I would not recommend the spontaneous method. Planning and scheduling are vitally important for business and commerce. Planning gives you structure and defines the goals you want to achieve. You just need to identify that line between planning and flexibility. Try to make your schedule freestyle so the universe can drop a couple of fun opportunities at you every once in a while. The very best plan you can make is a simple one. Think about how much Jesus could get done in a day and he never had an appointment book.

This is a habit that will take a little time to form. Become flexible in your plans and the way you live. Just taking this one concept and instilling it in your daily routine can get you off the treadmill. Don't let your life fall victim to overenthusiastic plans.

Silliness

From there to here, from here to there,
funny things are everywhere. Dr. Seuss

Silliness is one of the most obvious of the childlike traits. Silliness is an irrational form of entertaining yourself, and its sole purpose is to make you laugh. It's the ability to goof off harmlessly without regard for what people think. It can also lighten the load of so-called embarrassment. Like when you trip walking down the street and laugh at yourself instead of trying to cover up your mistake. Silliness can help break up a serious situation and cheer people up during tough times.

SILLY ARGUMENT STOPPER

I was working at Vancouver Television as a host in 1998. One morning in the office, two of the producers were having a top-quality shouting match regarding some insignificant detail. Whenever I tried to calm the situation down, it only made things worse. So I dropped my pants around my ankles and started crying about how all the yelling was scaring me. The director walked in and quickly realized what was happening, dropped his pants and began crying too. Soon everybody's pants were around their ankles, including the two antagonists, and the office had changed from toxic and uncomfortable to gut-wrenching laughter. Silliness can be used as a form of distraction from minor tragedies.

It's a way to have fun that costs nothing, feels good, makes others laugh and drives serious people bananas. Silliness is just a way of exercising your imagination and your sense of humor at the same time. The real key to silliness is getting past what other people think and putting fun first. Life is way too important to be taken seriously. People spend so much of their time and money trying to look unique, why not just be unique? Don't be afraid to be different.

Being silly is going off on tangents and great wild adventures in your imagination, your own form of personal happiness. Silliness is also personal in the sense that everyone has different levels of what they consider silly. We can all probably agree that the comedy troupe Monty Python is very silly. But some la-de-da businessman might find it silly to use a blue pen instead of a black pen on the year-end report. He might be able to make some sort of barnyard animal sound at the staff picnic but prancing around in a pink tutu might be a bit too much. For others, they can hardly wait to use the blue pen, make the animal sound and prance around in the tutu.

Silliness

Many people believe that showing signs of childlike sparkle will have them branded as intellectually challenged or having some kind of mental problem. Why is this childlike attitude considered stupid or a problem? To easily enjoy oneself is a problem? I mean, who cares what other people think about you enjoying your life anyway? Serious people think that everything must be taken seriously and every decision one makes must be a rational one. It's as if they will somehow be less of a person if they act out in a childlike manner. Why isn't seriousness or vanity considered a problem?

Now let's discuss the difference between being silly and looking silly. Being silly is proactively trying to entertain yourself or others. However, you may look silly when you're trying something new or attempting to navigate uncharted territory. We all look a little silly when we don't know what we're doing. There isn't a soul on the planet who has tried a new activity and avoided looking silly. Of course you will look silly–you may be clumsy or unsure of yourself or nervous. What do you think you were going to look like–a champion?

People who enjoy life will admire you and, yes, you will look silly but only to the people with the broomsticks up their butts. They're so caught up in knocking down everyone around them that they lose out on many possible joys. Don't take it personally if these people with the broomsticks up their butts label you as silly. Is it sillier to be silly or to have a broomstick up your butt? The broomstick is way more painful, or so I've heard.

No man is exempt from saying silly things; the mischief is to say them deliberately. Michel de Montaigne

You will do foolish things, but do them with enthusiasm. Sidonie Gabrielle Colette

Give yourself permission to act silly. Cast aside any concerns about what other people may think of you. You will need to suspend seriousness and judgment and go with the flow. If you want to be sane, sometimes you have to act a little crazy. Start small and work your way up. Sing and dance like nobody is watching. Give names to your car, your toaster or your favorite couch. Start by just being goofy around your plants, or when you're in the tub. Get in touch with your foolishness and let it all out. Phone your friends with silly voices and make them laugh. People talk silly to babies or dogs all the time. Why stop there? Like only babies or animals can enjoy that side of you?

Not Serious

Photos and home videos are a wonderful way to add hundreds of laughs to your life. Sure you can take the nice family portrait, but what about the fun photo too? The posed photo is such an unnatural facsimile of people. By making one goofy gesture in a photo, you can bring joy to so many people. Every single person who sees your photo album can smile and chuckle. What is the purpose of a photo anyway? To capture images of people. Why not capture an image of joy? Take that serious photo so that all the serious people know you can be serious. Take the fun photo as well so you can't be accused of being a stiff goat.

Play with kids, sing songs and make up your own words. Pretend you're the prime minister or the president and are in charge of the country. Watch senseless entertainment just for the fun of it. Play Twister or create crafts with materials you have on hand. Have a tickle trunk with fun hats, shirts and props. Change your identity daily!

Act silly with your lover. If you've been having sex the same way for the past four years, wouldn't a giggle or two liven it up? Why does sex have to be so serious? Why should a giggle wreck a romantic moment? Why can't it enhance it?

I have a friend (who I will let remain anonymous) who consistently brags about his silly sexual exploits. He and his girlfriend love to act out

everyday scenes like going to the bank or picking up the dry cleaning with the end result being fanatic intercourse. Act out your favorite love scene from a movie or TV. You be Cleopatra and I'll be Romeo. Maybe you want to videotape or try baby oil or blindfolds. Get silly and enjoy lovemaking like you've never thought possible.

There must be an atmosphere of silliness before you can execute it. If the silliness might create negative feelings in your environment, save it for another time. When tragedy strikes, being silly is usually not appropriate. Wearing a clown nose to a house fire and telling knock-knock jokes . . . hmm, I don't think so. Not every environment is willing to accept silly behavior, but if the car breaks down or you miss the bus, it might be a perfect time to get over your mini tragedy with a spot of silliness and get back to enjoying life.

Enjoy silliness when it comes into your day. I can never figure out why people can laugh at absurd things on the TV or movie screen but look at silliness with disgust when it's in public. Don't shun goofy people, be entertained by them. Enjoy the silliness of others even if you don't want to participate. Silliness could induce you to laugh so hard that snot comes out your nose.

I love being silly in public when a good Samaritan informs me how I should be acting. How should adults act? With long faces and boring conversations about the terrible state of our world? Scolding anybody having fun? Repressing playfulness as if it is a form of evil? How about developing cancer and heart disease at forty? Or working sixty hours a week? These things seem much more dangerous to me than a bit of silliness. A life without goofiness is life without oxygen or water. You can survive a short while without it, but sooner or later you shrivel up and turn into a dried-out bag of bones.

Though there is no scientific research, I believe that pent-up silliness causes plenty of avoidable depression and disease. Be stronger than the overpowering forces of Mind-Poo seriousness. Acting goofy rids you of any repressed absurdity that may have been building inside. Get in touch with your inner clown and go out into the circus of life.

Better a red face than a black heart. Old proverb

Laughing

Against the assault of laughter nothing can stand. Mark Twain

Your laugh is as unique as your voice and is the music of the soul. Laugh in the morning, giggle in the afternoon and chuckle in the middle of the night. Your smile should be running amok down at the park. It's not the most toys that wins, it's the most joys that wins. When you laugh with others, you become part of the crowd. It is contagious and only seems to generate more laughter around you–kind of a group happiness lubricant or social orgasm. It doesn't matter what corner of the world you come from or what color your skin is, laughter instantly brightens people up and makes them feel excellent. It is a universal language that everyone can relate to and appreciate.

The level of success in your life can be measured by your ability to laugh. Your mental health and all of your relationships, whether business or personal, should be ripe with laughter. If you have all the money, all the opportunity and all the stuff for a perceived successful life, but never laugh, what's the point? Some people are so blessed and yet they can't even crack a smile. If I had three Ferraris, an oceanfront home and three supermodel girlfriends, I don't think you would ever be able to get me to stop laughing. Why would anybody ever want success, fame, money or family if it didn't include fun, giggling and laughing?

Time spent laughing is time spent with the gods. Japanese proverb

Children intuitively know the benefits of a good laugh. That's why a child laughs an average of four hundred times a day while an adult's average is only fifteen. Some people laugh a lot, others less and some people never laugh at all. I know with all my heart that everybody has the ability to laugh.

This is another childlike skill that you already know how to do. When you laugh, you will not lose dignity or respect; you will only add to the sparkle of a situation. It can be highly addictive and once it begins, it can be very difficult to stop.

A two-minute belly laugh is equal to ten minutes on a rowing machine, so let it be part of your daily workout ritual. Doesn't laughing sound a lot more fun than sweating it out on a rowing machine? It relaxes your muscles, heightens your energy and alleviates your depression. Plain and simple, laughing is good for you.

Have you ever noticed exactly how you look and feel after a good laugh? You have a healthy glow in your face, your body looks limp and the look in your eyes suggests you've been floating out in the ozone somewhere. Laughing releases tension and endorphins. So that means you have your own little independent drug manufacturing plant inside your body. Why waste your money on caffeine, nicotine, headache pills or booze when you have an infinite supply of your own drugs? If you become addicted to this drug, you don't have to worry because you can never overdose on laughter or build up immunity to it. Start laughing and get those free drugs manufacturing.

Have you ever heard the saying, "Laughter is the best medicine"? I wonder–if it's the best medicine, why don't doctors prescribe it more often? Because if the sick and weak were told they could be healthier just by having more fun in their lives, who would the large drug companies manipulate?

Frowning makes you ugly. Maya Angelou

Laughter is also a great coping strategy. When times get tough, it will help you get through those difficult situations. For me, the more daunting my problems are, the more I need to laugh. It may not solve my problems, but at least I'm laughing. I have a couple of backups for the blues. I phone my friend Kevin or Erin or Stacey. They always make me laugh. I love watching "The Simpsons"–for me they are guaranteed laugh-producers. What or who makes you laugh? There is no shame in running to these solutions whenever you are feeling a little low.

Laughing will improve everything in your life–your career, friendships, love quotient, health and happiness. It makes you feel good, costs nothing and helps you deal with life's little challenges. So why in the world isn't everybody laughing?

Perhaps because our society doesn't really encourage laughter in a wide range of environments. When we were young, we were consistently reminded to grow up. Which really meant that the serious people were not impressed with all this gratuitous giggling. I was told not to laugh at school, at the dinner table or at the dinner party. Then, when I was out of school I was discouraged from laughing at work, on the bus or anywhere in public generally. It wasn't that there were signs saying no laughing allowed, but not very many people participate in the public giggle.

I remember a time when I was getting my driver's license renewed. The less-than-joyous government clerk thought that because I was so happy, I must be on drugs. All I was doing was being bright-eyed and bushy-tailed. This made me laugh even more, which got me thrown out of the office. I had to come back another time because Mrs. Crankypants believed the only way you could be happy in life was to be on drugs.

Why is laughter rarely encouraged in the street, at the workplace, in the grocery store or at the license bureau? What is up with all these no-laughter zones? Parties are OK but not at the breakfast table. It's as if laughter has to be given permission before it can appear. There are so many activities that are considered serious. Why, I ask, damn it, why?

It's good to laugh so hard you are worried about your safety.
Michael Eckford

A good place to start is to look at the mirror and snicker at the subject. Ease off on your drive for perfection and take a lighthearted approach to who you are. There are lots of things in this world you need to take seriously, but don't let yourself be one of them. You can be one of the best comedy shows on the planet. If you're feeling a little bit ugly, then have a laugh. So what if your nose is three feet long and you have eighteen chins–have a laugh. Maybe your bits lean to the left or the right–have a laugh. Maybe you have very close veins–have a laugh. We've become so hung up on what's wrong with ourselves that we've forgotten to enjoy what we have. Everybody has some kind of handicap, so you might as well make the best of it–have a laugh.

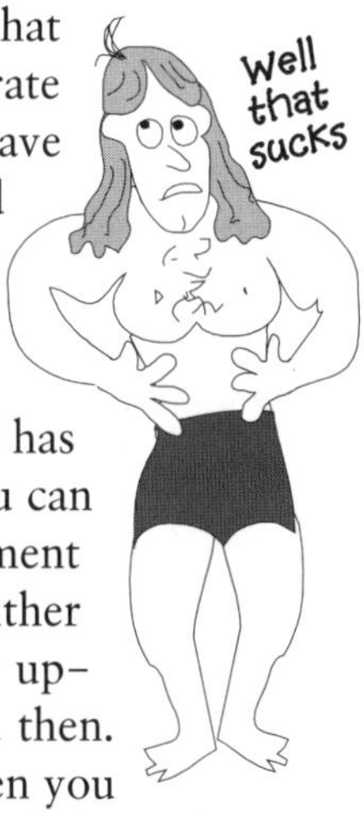

So you're not comfortable laughing at your body. What about your mistakes, shortcomings or quirky habits? Celebrate your uniqueness. Laughing at yourself doesn't mean you have to become the village idiot. Laughing at yourself should boost your self-confidence, not obliterate it.

Maybe there was a power outage and you ended up brushing with Preparation H. When I was in high school I tried to clear my sinuses with record cleaner. Everybody has experienced some kind of embarrassing moment. When you can learn to laugh at yourself, you are your own entertainment center. When your problems seem to compound, you can either get pissed off or you can just laugh. Don't beat yourself up–nobody is perfect. Even Fabio has a bad hair day now and then. When you laugh at yourself, everyone else will join in. When you see others laugh at themselves, how does that make you feel about them? I find it shows a humble, gentle side to people.

Who cares whether the glass is half full or half empty? Shouldn't the question be who has been drinking out of my glass? John Beiting

The ability to laugh easily is determined by your sense of humor. Your sense of humor gives you the capacity to appreciate the amusing side of life. You develop your "sense" of what is funny. Laughter is universal, but humor is in the eyes of the beholder. Just how amusing something is can be impossible to measure.

Through observation, you can learn to extract a lighthearted perspective and share it with the people around you. That's all comedians do–they have a different way of perceiving the world. After you practice this for a while it becomes easier and easier to see the humor beyond the front door.

You can consistently work towards improving your sense of humor and diversifying the list of things that make you laugh. While you develop your creativity, learning skills, playfulness, awareness, spontaneity, silliness and imagination, you will also be developing your sense of humor. A good sense of humor will open hundreds of doors, create many friendships, spark new relationships and keep you laughing zip-de-do-da-day.

He deserves Paradise who makes his companions laugh. The Koran

Everyone's sense of humor is different, and your humor may not always work the way you would like it to. Some people think Chris Rock is brilliant and others, like myself, can't stand the sound of his voice. It doesn't mean he isn't funny, he just isn't funny to me. The best comedian in the world cannot make 100 out of 100 people laugh. Don't expect everybody to see things the way you do; your sense of humor is your personal creation.

Developing your sense of humor will make it easier to produce a positive mood from a negative mood. If you have just discovered that you have cancer, it may not seem fitting to be happy about anything. There is nothing funny about this devastating illness, but your ability to laugh will help you cope. If you have only a short time to live, then why spend all your time weeping and complaining? You may not be able to control the fact that death has jumped the bus to your house, but you can control your mood. It may not save you, but it will certainly alleviate some of the suffering.

Now, it may not be death that's coming to visit, but it might be a false accusation, a car crash or a pink slip; whatever the tragedy, laughter will help. It's the cheapest way to help deal with your problems. When things are getting rough, why make them worse by becoming somber? If you fill your life with laughter, it will take your mind off the pain.

Laugh often, long and loud. Laugh until you gasp for breath or pee your pants. George Carlin

Think back to a time when it was easy for you to laugh. Is it OK if some of that natural laughter comes back? Look for humor and laughs in everyday situations. Hang out with people who make you laugh. You know, the kind of folks who are spreading their joyous melody of laughter to the world. Buy mindless toys that make you laugh.

The most wasted of all days is one without laughter. e.e. cummings

Telling jokes is another way of creating some chuckles. Some people are good at telling and others are better at listening. Keep a file of jokes you like. There are millions of ha-has on the Web that you can send around. Stay away from the racist and sexist jokes–you might get a laugh out of a racist, but you will just offend everyone else.

Movies and television are rich with laughter inspiration. National Lampoon, Monty Python, Austin Powers. You can laugh with children, who are funny without even trying. Learn what kinds of people and activities make you laugh, and then visit with them whenever you can. Laugh at your shortcomings, the state of the world, commercials, or books on how to have fun. Anything that needs to be laughed at should be laughed at.

Release negative emotions, boost your self-confidence and minimize your inhibitions. Be determined not to let another day go by without some form of laughter. Practice laughing for a few minutes each day. If nothing is funny, then fake it till you make it. The creator designed you to laugh, so laugh. Fun people use their good attitude to make it easy to laugh at the life they live. Give yourself permission to laugh whenever you feel like it and you could easily laugh four hundred times a day. Find out what tickles your funny bone and just keep tickling. A journey of a thousand smiles starts with a single giggle.

A funny monkey

Laughing is way more fun than anything. Shannon Wand

Friends

How rare and wonderful is that flash of a moment when we realize we have discovered a friend. William E. Rothschild

You can have all the money in the world; you can have a rewarding career and do numerous fun things, but if you have nobody to share these moments with, you have nothing. Good friends are invaluable and absolutely necessary to leading a happy, fulfilling life.

What is a friend anyway? A friend is someone who knows everything about you, good or bad, and still cares for you. They support you in times of weakness, and pole-vault you in times of joy. True friendships are based on mutual respect, giving and support. Friendships are intertwined with honesty, loyalty and unconditional acceptance. They are non-clinging and non-dependent. Add in compassion, intimacy, affection, thoughtfulness and the ability to warm your heart on the coldest of days.

Many people fill their lives with nice companions, but when the chips are down these so-called friends are running in the other direction. You need people in your life who can offer you a form of spiritual intimacy. Someone willing to come over and support you when everyone else has left. Friends will come and go–it is a fact of life. When you have a friend who stays around in good times and bad, you are very lucky.

Real friends won't use you as an emotional dump to ventilate their latest batch of distressing emotions. Real friends are not asking you for favors all the time, they are not spending your money and they are not donating endless advice on what is wrong with your life. If people are hanging with you because of external benefits like wealth or power, they are not friends. They are butt kissers. I am not suggesting you dump your friends at the first sign of these qualities, but don't hang onto users and abusers. Friends are there to help you grow, to bring you pleasure and to make you a better person.

When we do have some less-than-perfect friends, getting rid of them may not be an easy task. You may have grown up on the same street or gone to school together. Maybe you went through some tough times like a war or a natural disaster. Loyalty is important, but you have to ask yourself, "Is this person still adding to my life or are they taking away from it?" If they are all take and no inspiration, it is time to let them go.

You can have more fun shoveling cow poop with a quality friend than you can going to Disneyland with a whiner.

Stop calling friends who bring you down. The world is full of moaners and groaners, and it's best that they hang out with one another. By all means help your friends when they need your help. But you are not obligated to listen to people's misery until the end of time. Plan a way to get out of the relationship if it is not allowing you to smile and grow.

When they confront you about your lack of attention, be very careful in your response. Telling them they are ruining your life might not be the best thing to do. If they are someone that you can communicate with, let them know how their behavior has been affecting you. Remember that they have just tuned into some Mind Poo, and it is not them that is the problem but the way they have been acting. If you don't think the truth will work, you may need to stretch the truth a bit. Tell them you have been busy at work or that you need to spend more time with your spouse. Say whatever it takes so they can walk away feeling good about themselves and you can be free of their negativity. If you stop calling them, sooner or later they will go away.

Getting out is easy; it's deciding to get out that is the tough part. If your friends are not right for you, then let them go. If you see traits like dishonesty, manipulation, guilt or any other happiness-robber, then get away from them immediately. Throw their number out and forget where they live. If your friends are taking away from your happiness, they are not really

true friends. There are plenty of great people out there; you don't have to hang out with tree stumps. Kindly and gently get rid of the people who do not add to your life.

Maybe you are satisfied with your friends already. You already have a happy friend or two, but why not have five or ten? For you to pursue this life of fun, you will need to be constantly supported and surrounded by as many positive people as possible. Misery loves company but so does happiness.

So how can you expand the quality of your friendship portfolio? First make a commitment to excellence. You can only have deep friendships with deep people–if you try to have a solid relationship with an insincere person, it just won't work. I am not suggesting you ditch your friends at the first sign of trouble, but you certainly don't have to put up with a bunch of crap either. Stand up for yourself by choosing your playmates carefully and never sell yourself short.

My best friend is the one who brings out the best in me.
Henry Ford

A few years back I had a huge turning point in my life. A so-called friend had just chewed me out because he thought the spiritual weekend retreat I had just attended was a scam, and he was most upset about it. In that moment I decided I would only have people in my life who supported my life instead of attempting to destroy it. If your friends are disrespectful to you, cutting you off in conversations and insensitive to your needs and wants, they are not your friends. They may have been at one time but not any more. I kicked him out of my house and never called him again.

I mentally went through my list of friends and discovered that none of my day-to-day friends were helping me at all. There was no inspiration, no mutual love or support. Just pub pals and people I killed time with. I realized the difference between friendliness and friendship. They were all friendly but none of them were friends, so I stopped calling all of them.

I went almost two years without any kind of friendship, but you know what? In the process of getting rid of the old skanky pals, I made room in my life for quality friends. I spent a lot of time trying to find out who I really was and what was important to me. I learned that my friends were usually a good reflection of how I was and that I had attracted all of them. Once I began to improve, so did the kind of people who were showing up in my life. Now I have plenty of wonderful, heart-warming friendships. If I hadn't done that evaluation and committed to being a better person who was surrounded by quality people, I would still be getting yelled at for how I live my life.

Once you have committed to deleting the skanky pals, the next step to getting a friend is to be a friend. Don't look for what you can get in your new relationships, look for what you can give. Friendship can be free in a monetary sense, but you will have to pay a price. Everything that you try to get out of a friendship, you will need to give back double.

Outside of a dog, a book is man's best friend.
Inside of a dog it's too dark to read. Groucho Marx

Think of how you like to be treated and then treat the people around you the same way. Have integrity right from the beginning. Never back-stab a friend and make your word your bond. Avoid gossip at all costs. Don't speak of it, don't listen to it and don't participate in it. Formulate promises sparingly and always keep them no matter what the cost.

Be open and honest with people, put your heart into every hand you shake, look for common ground not differences, smile and say hello to the people in your life. Ask them about their family, where they are from, where they live, their hobbies. Learn how to make people feel important. Learn to listen to people. Not just the words but also the true message that comes through in their tone of voice and facial expressions.

Charm is a way of getting the answer yes without having asked any clear question. Albert Camus

When you are friendly with people, it will pay off in the real world. People will be nicer to you. Sales clerks will go out of their way to check the back room to see if there is a special deal. It might be a good parking spot or getting out of a speeding ticket. It might work, it might not, but at least you're adding to the world instead of being a snot head. Think how good it feels when someone treats you right. Not only will being friendly make your day more pleasant, it will open more doors for you than you can ever imagine. Being mean to people will close nearly every door on the planet.

Meeting new people can be challenging. We are living closer to one another than ever before, stacked on top of each other in apartment buildings, but we never talk to one another besides the odd "good morning." We have gated communities, fences and walls to separate us in our closeness, but wonderful, joyous people are in every corner and every neighborhood on the planet. Go to social events, take up a new sport, hang out at the coffee shop. Join clubs, say hello to people, do charity work. March your butt into the world so that you can broadcast your intentions of finding some new friends.

Seek out friendship diversity. If you are an engineer and all your friends are engineers, your chances of having conversations about something other than engineering may be limited. Look for other points of view–get young friends, old friends, friends with different political and religious views. Interesting friends make for interesting encounters. Think of new ways to combine recreation ideas, travel, fitness and friendship. Make a real effort to smile at everyone you meet. Pursuing fun activities will help you get close to other people. Having fun with others promotes healthy, happy relationships. A bond that is forged in delight will be etched into your heart forever.

I would rather have a million friends than a million dollars.
Edward Vernon Rickenbacker

When you are out looking, you may not always connect on the same wavelength, but if you are out in the marketplace, sooner or later you are going to succeed. Keep looking for connections with other humans. Say hi, smile–do whatever it takes. If you find someone that you think could be a possible friend, this is what you do:

Don't wait for them to call you, pick up the phone and invite them out for a coffee. When you are with them, listen, not just with your ears but with your eyes and heart as well. You will find it much easier to make friends by getting interested in them than by trying to get them interested in you. Don't brag about anything–I mean, besides your ego, who cares how great you think you are? Let your actions speak louder than your words. Don't impress–be impressed.

Make a kind gesture; get some tickets for a sporting event or a play. Make some plans to do fun things together. Make the initial effort and if they have no response, then you know what to do. Next! If they fail to see what a wonderful person you are, you may as well move on and find someone who can.

You may have some existing friendships that have fallen by the wayside. A good friendship will need maintenance much like your car. Occasionally, you will have to change the oil and give it a tune-up. Maybe you need to give it a warm, soapy bath and rub in a little Turtle wax. Forgive those stupid little things that have come between you in the past. Remember why you were friends in the first place. Keep in touch, write a letter or make a call to go for coffee.

Remind the people that are your good friends why you love them as much as you do. On September 11 I phoned every one of my friends and reminded them how much I appreciate them being in my life. Then I wondered why I had to wait for such a terrible incident to motivate me to let my appreciation be known. Tell your friends you care right now. Stop reading, put the book down, step away from the book and call someone.

In my circle of friends, every person has many outstanding traits, but there always seems to be one trait they are masters of. It may be patience or kindness, thoughtfulness or loyalty. Every time I notice one of these master traits, I thank the universe for bringing me such a great teacher as well as a great friend. The diversity of your friends will make you a more dynamic character.

Friends are an absolute blessing that can provide infinite joy for you. What kind of people are you around now? Your friends are usually a pretty good reflection of who you are. Are you hanging out with a few quality eagles or a flock of conformist, butt kissing chickens? Stay away from the chickens and go fly with the eagles. You can never have too many eagles flapping around. When it feels as if the world is out to get you, your friends will be there for support. Be patient; good friendships don't happen overnight.

The statistics on sanity are that one out of every four Americans is suffering from some form of mental illness. Think of your three best friends. If they're okay, then it's you.
Rita Mae Brown

Expectations

A great obstacle to happiness is to expect too much happiness.
Anonymous

High expectations are very important for your earth visit. They are like a target, something to look forward to–a desired result. It is the catalyst that challenges you to be the best you can be. If you set high expectations, more often than not you will get results close to what you expect. Good expectations are a way of saying, this is where I am going and when I see this I will be pleased. Bad expectations are projecting that things will not work out and then you can say, "I told you so" when your life falls apart.

Whether you realize it or not, expectations have infiltrated every part of your life. You have expectations about your work, your performance, your peers, your family, the cable company, the mail service, the police, politicians, your vacation, your car ... everything. You expect your phone to work, the cops to catch the robbers and your paycheck to be ready when it is supposed to be.

The problem is not having high expectations, the problem is when your expectations are not met. More than likely you feel a sense of disappointment or even anger. If you are expecting the driver ahead of you to drive the speed limit and he doesn't, what happens? What if the red light at the intersection never changes–do you feel giggly inside or not giggly?

We project numerous expectations onto our lovers and spouses. We expect them to take us away from sadness and deliver us to gladness. There could be sexual expectations or financial expectations. If you expect your lover to be monogamous and they end up sleeping with the neighbor, the boss and the pizza delivery person, you will probably be a little miffed.

When dealing with your expectation of others, the way to minimize disappointment is to convey your expectations. When your expectations are not met, divulge your disappointment in the most gentle, dignified way possible. We all hope that telepathy will solve all of our communication problems. If you don't disclose clearly what is expected, people can only guess what makes you happy.

Pointing out your expectations is important to all facets of your life. In the work world, whether you are the boss or the employee, it will go a long way to minimizing miscommunication. You don't have to go through life guessing what is expected of you. If you are ever unsure, just ask people: What exactly do you expect of me? Make sure you completely understand, and when you need to describe your expectations, make sure they thoroughly understand. If they never tell you what is expected of you and vice versa, both parties are involved in an expectation crapshoot.

Some expectations can never be fulfilled no matter what happens. There will always be people who have unreasonable expectations of you with total disregard for how you feel about it. Some parents want their child to grow up to be the best kid on the planet–to marry someone they approve of and do exactly what they tell them to do, such as take a certain career path. Maybe your mother was a doctor and she expects you to be one too. The problem is that you faint at the sight of blood. Or they could want you to run the family dry-cleaning business, but you hate the chemicals. It doesn't make you a bad person if you don't live up to their expectations. It's their expectations that are the problem, not you.

We inevitably doom our children to failure and frustration when we try to set their goals for them. Dr. Jess Lair

Society expects you to have the best car, the best home and the best stereo system. And if you don't have all these things and a relationship with a perfect lover, then somehow you are a failure. If you are out there enjoying your life, doing the very best you can, who cares what kind of car you drive or if you drive? The size of your house does not dictate whether you are a good person or not. If society, your families and friends were more concerned with what makes you happy rather than what makes them happy, it would leave you a lot more room to be a joyful person.

Our fragile little egos expect that everybody we meet will like us. But not everyone will love you no matter how hard you try. That would be an unreasonable expectation. We have unreasonable expectations of perfection for our lovers, our friends, our jobs, our day-to-day lives and ourselves. Looking for perfection is a recipe for anxiety. You can never be perfect at anything and neither can anybody else.

Setting unreasonable expectations for your job, your career or your relationships is asking for trouble. Unreasonable expectations cause two things to happen. One is that if they're too high you will never reach them because you don't believe they are possible. Two is that when your expectations are not met, you will certainly be disappointed. If you expect to have good weather, you will become disappointed when it rains. When our expectations have not been met, we cannot change the situation but we can change our perception.

Equipment breaks down, the skies will spit rain, bad things happen and lovers forget to pick up the milk. If we can find that fine balance between expecting the best and staying open and flexible if the "worst" happens, confronting unmet expectations will be a lot easier. Make no mistake about it, having high expectations is important to a healthy lifestyle. But sometimes having high expectations can be both a blessing and a hindrance.

I was down at the grocery store the other day and the clerk was complaining about her holidays. "I had such an awful time on my vacation. The key didn't work for my hotel room and I had to call maintenance three times." She had this look of disappointment that made her face scowl. This clerk spent seven days in Cancun on a beautiful beach in the Caribbean Sea. She had plenty of fun and food and relaxation. She had a problem for fifteen minutes at her hotel with a key. That one little incident ruined her vacation.

So her "Door Expectations" were not met and she stayed pissed about the key issue for weeks. What do you think would have happened if she had said, "I expect to enjoy myself no matter what happens"? Do you think she would still be whining about the key problem or would she have just let it pass and forgotten all about it? She probably didn't read the instructions on the travel brochure, which specifically said, "Relax and enjoy yourself."

If she'd been really open to the moment and to the synchronicities in life, she might have made good friends with the maintenance person. He might have invited her to spend time with his family. Or he might have led her to learn more about Cancun and the people and rich culture of Mexico. Who knows? Next time she returned to Mexico she might have had an open invite to stay with the family. Everything happens for a reason. That key "problem" might have been there to unlock some block she had to discover more about herself and her purpose in life, but her expectations for perfection helped to slam the door shut.

If you set high expectations in your life, that's good, just don't beat yourself up if they're not achieved. When you go to a fancy restaurant and the service is lousy, don't blow your top. Maybe the stove broke down, the cook was late or your server just lost a friend to illness. Be understanding and get over it. When you take this attitude and everything goes to hell in a handbasket, you will still be able to have a great time.

I expect nothing. I fear no one. I am free.
Nikos Kazantzakis

Another way of looking at this is setting good intentions before you set high expectations. Setting your intentions lays the groundwork for better results. If your intentions are to enjoy life no matter what happens, then setting your expectations high will help drive you towards your good intentions. Always keep your intention clear. Then, when you are planning and setting your expectations and they are not met, you can always fall back on your good intentions.

When setting your expectations, avoid setting them so high that you could never see it happening–it has to happen in your head before it will happen in reality. When Olympians win gold they expect it. They don't say, "I hope I win," they say, "I will win." That kind of expectation drives them to train and focus properly. Great athletes intend to do the best in whatever they do. When their target is not met, they're proud that they have put in their best effort.

Fun people expect things to work out, but if life takes a detour, they're open to enjoying and learning from the process regardless of what happens. Expect to laugh and have a really good time. If your adventure or event doesn't work out, then your playful, fun attitude will still make it great. Expect to chuckle, giggle and enjoy your way throughout every single day.

If you expect a book like this to give you answers to your dilemmas, you will probably find them. You get what you expect and if you expect something or someone to be a pain in the butt, pretty soon you will have hemorrhoids. If you expect to fail, you will. Without expectation and hope, there can be no progress. If you are setting unrealistic expectations, you will be disappointed. When your expectations fall short, the trick is to improvise and make the best of what you have. Keep your intention for joy strong and in the front of your mind. You are the captain of your ship and you need to take charge of your intentions and clarify your expectations. You have the power, so turn on the switch.

Expect everything and anything seems nothing. Expect nothing and anything seems everything. Samuel Hazo

Judging

Never judge a book by its cover. Really old saying

We are trained from birth to judge more facets of our life than we care to admit. We judge our friends, our neighbors, our co-workers, what people wear, what people worship, ourselves–it never ends. We use every belief, past experience and bit of knowledge to judge what is in front of us. We do it at lightning speed, too. In five seconds we have determined whether we like someone or not and we always believe that our judgments are right. When you make up your mind before you know all the facts, it restricts your freedom, quashes your ability to learn and gives you a distorted perception. Judging is a kind of "fun antimatter" that causes us to miss out on plenty of opportunities and friendships.

Human beings have a need to compartmentalize everything. Good or bad, white or black, wet or dry. We feel compelled to make somebody right and make somebody wrong. We are quick to criticize and condemn. The notion that picking a side is more important than understanding both sides is ingrained in our heads during our entire upbringing.

We hate what we don't understand. If it's not the way we are, then it must be below the grade. Generalizations are then generously supplied, which have no basis in reality. All teenagers are bad or all Muslims are terrorists. We use negative judgments as a pathetic attempt to enhance our sense of worth and make other people look terrible.

Who's to say which religion is right, which politics are right, what activities are right or what fashions are right? Diversity is the only thing we have in common. If we were all the same, why would we want to get to know other people? If people want to wear turbans or pierce their tongues or try on a toupee–whatever–what does it matter as long as it doesn't interfere with you personally? Why waste your time trying to change people who don't even know you exist? Wouldn't you rather watch a sunset or be playing golf or whatever it is you like to do?

Every person on this planet has a purpose and it is important to the big picture. Accepting the world as it is, and people as they are, will liberate all kinds of energy for you to go out and enjoy life. Fun people accept their fellow earth dwellers with a live-and-let-live attitude. They are not concerned with what is the right way because they realize that people have every right to do whatever they want. Happiness mongers accept their own individuality and can't be bothered spending their time judging what other people are doing. They would rather learn about other people and their rituals because they may be missing out on some great personal entertainment moments.

Most people are under the illusion that they can see the world exactly the way it is, but each of us sees this world from our own point of view. If you think your ways are right, you might go around trying to fix the world. And if that's your calling in life, then get out there and help make some changes. If you're just whining because you think you know everything, then you will only be a whiner. Just let the world exist for what it is because riding the rails of righteousness is a very tiring job. Your displeasure over external things exists only because you have let your judgments dictate your feelings.

The average man's judgment is so poor, he runs a risk every time he uses it.
Edgar Watson Howe

Half the time we make misinformed judgments. Where has the information come from? From a gossipy friend, a stranger, the media? What if the friend was angry at the time and exaggerated for the sake of telling a good story. What if the stranger had a hidden agenda? Anytime you fail to see both sides of the coin, you are making a clouded judgment. And usually whatever judgment we make first we will fight for tooth and nail. Do like the professional judges do. Get all the facts from both sides before making a judgment. Better yet, don't make a judgment at all. Unless you're being paid to judge, why work for free?

When people judge you, realize that they are probably only seeing you for a small portion of the day. You are with yourself all the time so don't you think you have a better perception of who you really are? If you know you're a good person, then screw them and their misinformed judgments. Nobody is accepted by everyone. Why should you be worrying about the odd misguided soul? Just be yourself and live your life. No matter what you do, some people may criticize and ridicule you. That's their problem

If you are an egotistically challenged person, it may be important to know what other people think, but it's still irrelevant. You are never going to please everybody and you never can. If you send a hundred people to a movie, some will love it and some will hate it. This goes for music, food, clothes or lifestyles. People are different and so are their tastes. So question people's judgments about you and realize it is their issues they are dealing with, not yours. If you don't like to be unfairly judged, why do it to others?

When someone cuts you off in traffic, you get angry. Matter of fact, you become so angry that you need to set this person straight. How do you think they will respond? "Oh, wow, he is yelling at me very loud, he must be very smart. I will correct my behavior immediately!" But what if you get out of your car and tell him that his mother was a goat-kisser? It turns out his mother has only an hour to live and he's trying to get to the hospital. You feel like dog poop. It's rare that you ever get the full story so until you do, chill out and just let people be.

Any fool can criticize or complain–and most fools do.
Dale Carnegie

Now judging yourself, that's a different matter. We are so quick to judge what is wrong with us we forget what is right with us. If judging people means boosting your self-esteem by making somebody look terrible, what happens when you judge yourself? How can you boost your self-esteem and degrade yourself at the same time? Seems silly, doesn't it? If you have a habit of negatively judging yourself, give yourself a pat on the head. You're a well-trained dog. Ruff, ruff.

Take it easy on yourself and while you're at it, take it easy on the world. Honor other people's religions, careers and lives. The way to stop judging is to learn acceptance, and acceptance is gained through knowledge and compassion. Treat people with dignity instead of disdain. It's a lot easier to agree with someone when you take the time to find out where they are coming from. Try honestly to see the world from another person's point of view. Put yourself in their shoes because they probably have something valuable to share with you. Instead of looking at what's wrong with people, try to find out what's right. Embrace words like understanding, respect and tolerance.

Fun people understand that everybody is different and that everyone enjoys different things. They never take offense at the fact that you don't like the kind of games they play. They will enthusiastically tell you about them and encourage you to play, but if you don't want to they will just move on to find someone else to play with. They would never put someone in an uncomfortable position just for the sake of fun. For example, some people like to sing in public while others would rather pull their own teeth out. Fun people realize that what is fun for some is pure misery for others.

People take different roads to seek happiness. Just because they are not on your road doesn't mean they are going the wrong way. Instead of judging their lives, you could support their love of collecting fish nostrils. To broaden your happiness you must respect people for who they are and what they enjoy. Can you imagine a dog ridiculing another dog because it wouldn't play fetch?

Avoid finding fault with anybody, no matter how easy it seems. Go a whole day without judging anyone. The more you stop judging and allow others to be free, the more you can be free. Bring happiness and joy to people as you journey through life. Live your life by your rules and what is right for you. As you begin to accept the people of this planet, you can expect a good portion of your misery to disappear into thin air. Just because everyone else judges this world and everything in it, it doesn't mean you have to.

A closed mouth gathers no foot. Anonymous

Competition

Just play. Have fun. Enjoy the game. Michael Jordan

Competition has infiltrated our lives. It starts in school and is nurtured throughout our time on this earth. We are competitive in our jobs, with our neighbors and with our friends. Healthy competition is great; it drives you to try a little harder, to be a little more. In sports, you can learn about teamwork through competition, develop the ability to think on your feet or strengthen your body athletically. Competitiveness in business causes you to make your products or services cheaper, better and faster.

But being competitive can bring out the best and worst in people. Competition is like spice. It can add zest, but too much can leave a bad taste in your mouth. Too much focus on winning will take the fun right out of the event. If you're a competitive person, this chapter may not make sense, but just hear me out.

What is the purpose of a game? To play or to win? When you are addicted to winning, you create a lot of losers. It seems like we are all trying to win the rat race, but the winner of that race is a rat. Is that what you're really aiming for? Western culture teaches us to win, but it's hard to have fun at a game when your only goal is to beat everyone else.

Organized sports for kids are huge in North America. Baseball, football, basketball and hockey are the big ones. Parents invest plenty of time and money in their children's sports. Some want their kids to become superstars; others just want them to have the chance to play with their friends. Some parents love getting their kids involved in something positive; others have started fist fights with each other while watching in the stands.

That's where competition crosses the line of fun. When the desire to win becomes the only purpose of playing the game, the fun doesn't get a chance to participate. Do you think Mother Teresa, Jesus and Buddha were competing to see who could save the most souls? They probably weren't concerned about what the competition was doing. They just wanted to do their best to help people.

You can say that competition is a natural thing and you would be 100 percent right. Animals do it all the time. Look at bucks or rams smashing heads together and goring each other's guts out. Yes, there will always be winners and losers, but do we have to gore each other's guts out deciding? Yes, competition is part of the natural law. You see it everywhere, in politics, in professional sports, in the game of life.

As long as I can focus on enjoying what I'm doing, having fun, I know I'll play well. Steffi Graf

If intense competition is prevalent in your life, you will notice that glimpses of pleasure only appear when you crush your opponent. Fun people do not become obsessed with winning, they become obsessed with enjoying healthy competition. Do you remember a time when you went out with all your little friends and just played for the sake of playing? What did it feel like? Children don't care if they win or lose, they just want to play. They aren't concerned about how they look on the court or crushing their opponents. They don't use rule books; they use the spirit of play as the rules.

I like to play competitively, but I also just like to play. If I manage to make a great play against a competitor in a sporting game that's fantastic, but if they become obsessed with trying to get revenge for my maneuver then it is no longer fun. The classic example is when a professional team is losing or just about to lose a game and they try cheap shots and fighting to prove their worth. Too bad, too late, you already lost. Being a good competitor also means having great sportsmanship skills.

I have given up trying to beat people at games all the time. If you beat all the people all the time, nobody will ever want to play with you. Having fun is about connecting with other people, not proving how good you are. I am more interested in having my lovers, my friends or my guests experience joy than experience defeat. If you must compete to win, there will always be a time and a place for you to do it in a serious fashion.

A short while ago two of my favorite friends invited my neighbor and me over for a card game. There was no money involved, just four pals dealing out the deck. When my neighbor forgot to show her winning cards before she shuffled, voices were raised and the rules were laid out. It was an innocent mistake, but it was perceived as deceitful. It wasn't like we were playing the World Series of Hearts, but to my friends it sure was.

NOT SO FUN CARD GAME

If you make every game a life and death proposition, you're going to have problems. For one thing, you'll be dead a lot. Dean Smith

She made a mistake and our friendly get-together went from fun card game to a serious situation. There was a sense of mistrust in the air, and their need to win surpassed any other fun we could have discovered. The spirit of play had been drop-kicked out of my chest. I couldn't understand what the big deal was. Sure you want to play by the rules so it is fair for everyone. But when the spirit of the rules overcomes the spirit of fun, then it's not a game I want to play.

You don't have to play games that require a winner or a loser. It is impossible to have a bad game of tag or poor water-fighting skills. When you play games that require keeping score, all you're doing is comparing your skills to your competitor's. You don't have to keep score all the time. Sometimes you can play just for the sake of playing. I used to hate golf, but now that I no longer keep score I have a great time. I can swing forty-seven times on the same shot and it just doesn't matter. Don't let your life or your games be overshadowed by rules and regulations.

Even if there are rules, it doesn't mean you have to use them. Adapt the rules in whatever game you're playing to maximize the enjoyable parts. If you are playing tennis against someone who has a very poor serve–could you overlook a couple of bad serves to keep the game going? Twist the rules to fit your needs. What if your rookie opponent never hits it in bounds? You could call every foul ball and win a crushing defeat or you could return them and say nothing.

When showing people new activities or sports, your goal is not to show them how good you are and how poor they are. I can never understand an experienced skier who takes a new skier down terrain that is impossible for the rookie to negotiate. The rookie ends up walking down and crying. Hmmm, nice friend. When you're showing people new activities, you have to treat them like crystal; they are very fragile and they could break. If you fail to do this, you have actually hurt or even scarred them for life concerning that activity. Is that the result you want?

For when the One Great Scorer comes to mark against your name, He writes–not that you won or lost–but how you played the Game. Grantland Rice

Now when it comes to the actual act of winning, make sure you do it in a humble manner. Shrug it off as luck. Lighten the sting of your victory on your competitors. You don't need to brag about anything because you've already won. If you've worked hard for it and you need to celebrate, do it away from whomever you beat. Why would you want to make them feel worse? If you overcelebrate, you look like a real ass.

Give them a few words of consolation about how hard they tried and how much effort it took to beat them. Learn to praise your competitors

behind their backs. Take them for a beer. Even if they didn't win the game, at least they can go home feeling good about themselves and the company they keep.

Be quick to congratulate your opponents when you are beaten. Shake hands when you are done. Brag to others about what a great job they did at beating you. Pride yourself on your sense of fair play. Do not use excuses or blame anybody for the loss. They were just better than you on that particular day–nothing more, nothing less. If you pout about your loss, you look like a crybaby.

One thing that I love about the game of rugby is the prevalence of good sportsmanship. It is very common for two rugby teams that have played together to go out for beers after a game. What does that say about the losers? What does that say about the winners? If you ask me, it makes them all winners.

Winning is a cheap high that doesn't last. When you can learn to celebrate losing as much as you do when you win, you will be destined to a life of happiness. Winning isn't always finishing first, sometimes it's just finishing. Loving life, win or lose, will bring you infinite joy. Avoid sayings like winning at all cost. Sounds expensive to me.

You find that you have peace of mind and can enjoy yourself, get more sleep, and rest when you know that it was a 100 percent effort that you gave–win or lose. Gordie Howe

Health & Healing

A man's health can be judged by which he takes two at a time– pills or stairs. Joan Welsh

A healthy body will give you the opportunity to take on life full steam. Fun people are generally healthy, fit and willing to get off the couch. I have met many fun people who are not physically fit, but their options were limited. If you have to carry an extra fifty or hundred pounds around, your physical encounters with fun will be restricted. You can have money, friends and a wonderful family, but if you aren't taking care of your body, you're in for unnecessary unhappiness.

Your body is the tool that allows you to experience physical fun. It isn't necessary to be in Olympic-class shape, but some level of fitness will expand your opportunities. Reclaim the vitality and energy you already have–it is sequestered by fast food and laziness. If you don't exercise, you'll soon discover that you begin to rust and rot. Your body was designed to move–so move. Your lack of activity may not show up as a disability right away, but sooner or later it will catch up to you.

Why is it that some seventy-year-olds can run marathons and some use a cane? The more you exercise, eat nutritious foods and rest up, the more energy and good feelings you will have. The more you sit on your couch, eat potato chips and whine, the more miserable your life will be. Think about how you want to look, weigh and feel. Then figure out the steps you need to get there. Sometimes people go out and make unrealistic goals: This week I will a) start running; b) give up drinking, smoking, caffeine and sugar; c) start a weight-lifting program; d) rid myself of all other bad habits. Then when our expectations aren't met, we consider ourselves big fat losers because we can't immediately break a cycle of behavior that took years to develop.

I like long walks, especially when they are taken by people who annoy me. Fred A. Allen

Fun people, on the other hand, stay fit by being involved in physical activities that give them pleasure. You could go biking, hiking, skiing, walking, swimming, or you could play hockey, basketball or soccer. Why go work out when you could go play out? Maybe you enjoy tennis or golf or kayaking? Now you have even more reasons to go out and play. Exercise releases built-up tension, much like a soft car wash for your soul. It heals, rebuilds and injects excitement into your daily routine.

Participating in fun activities that include cardiovascular effort is far more enjoyable than going to the gym to work out. A workout sounds like work to me. Why be around a bunch of sweaty egos under fluorescent lights and loud disco music when you could be on top of a mountain conquering the planet? Take up activities that are fun and losing weight will be fun. It is way better than battling it with a robot walker machine watching CNN and the daily death count. Combine your entertainment and your exercise.

But you say, "I don't have the energy to get out there and climb those mountains." It all starts with baby steps. Go for a fifteen-minute walk every day. Sign up for some fun activities in your community. As you do more, you will build success upon success and eventually you will be healthy. You want your cardiovascular system to be prepared for whatever fun opportunity arises.

When you start to physically play, you also begin to get rid of excess weight. Losing weight can be extremely difficult, but you only have to do it one ounce at a time. Turn your weight-loss mission into a reason to get out there and enjoy life. We were originally designed to look for food and shelter, not to sit on our derrieres and eat potato chips.

If you're going to play and have fun, proper nutrition is your only option. With the easy availability of fast foods we have become a nation of portion overachievers and nutritional underachievers. Smart marketing has convinced us that changing our diet to food that is good for us will result in deprivation. "Oh, no," we think to ourselves, "we're missing out on all the good things." What's so good about heart disease and premature death? If that's what those kinds of foods give you, why not eat real foods that give you energy, put a spring in your step and let you sleep well?

Eat more vegetables, drink plenty of water and stay away from fattening foods. Chew on fruit instead of junk food, and drink juice instead of soda. Stay away from heavy sauces (why do you think they call them heavy?). Cut down or eliminate sugar, cigarettes, alcohol, white bread and chemicals in your food. Maybe your body can't digest dairy or wheat products. Don't be afraid of being called a "health nut"; it's a lot better than being called a "fat nut." Besides, what's so nutty about giving your body foods that let it operate at its maximum potential? We're convinced that we're missing out on something when we adjust our diet. What are you missing out on because of poor health and fitness levels? Quality food will help you feel great and age gracefully.

It was recently discovered that research causes cancer in rats. Unknown

Sure it's way easier to drink beer, eat ice cream and grow your butt than it is to get healthy. Fast food crap stores are on every corner in America. We're inundated with advertising that drives the message deep into our brain to eat the crappiest food possible. Fast food marketers have no interest in keeping you healthy–they want to sell you as much lousy food as you will buy. They want you to supersize your drink so you can supersize your bum.

BRAINSTORMING IN BURGER HEADQUARTERS

If you want to know more, there are about a million books available on the subject. Get more information and then make an informed decision. I am not a nutritional expert so you need to spend a little time researching what foods you should be eating. Your body knows best what foods are best

for you. Maybe you just need to eat a little less at each meal, until you are reasonably full. You don't have to overeat at Christmas or Thanksgiving or any other opportunity. Eat more rabbit food–why do you think they can run so fast?

Take responsibility for your body weight. Don't blame it on anybody or anything. Exercising more and eating less will take you farther than any excuse ever will. I remember watching a story on television about a 130-pound three-year-old. His obese mother was crying because no doctor could help her. During the story, they showed the little gaffer playing in the living room. Bowls of chips and cheese puffs surrounded him and he was stuffing his fat little face with his fat little fingers. Mom (no lightweight herself) continued to tell the camera about how tough it was being ridiculed when she took her child to the local burger place. I don't think she even considered that the food choices available to her son were fattening him up.

I guess I don't so much mind being old, as I mind being fat and old. Peter Gabriel

If you don't take care of yourself physically and emotionally, you will end up sick, and sick days will cut into your play days. It is not normal to have two or three bad colds every year. Little germs and bugs are everywhere and when your immune system is working well, they just pass you by. Ask yourself, "What is it that is making me so sick and how can I get healthy?" Your body knows the answer to that question.

It may be more than your diet and exercise levels. If you are experiencing excessive stress and Mind Poo, you will become ill. Figure out how to get rid of stress. It will cause nothing but ulcers and constipation of your fun. It is a psychological poison that cannot be ignored.

When you do become sick, the first step is to accept it. You are not the sickness, it is merely a guest. Gently ask your illness why it came to visit and what you can do to allow it to leave. Sickness is nature's way of saying take it easy for a week or twenty. Sometimes an illness can make you slow down and rethink your entire life. Fail to take care of your body and it will simply go on strike.

The earth will not go into a holding pattern if you are sick for a day. Erma Bombeck

When you are sick, STOP and get healthy again. Do not compromise on your health because it is your ticket to Funsville. Try to discover what it is that has made you ill. Sometimes it is a simple solution. Take a look at heartburn. If you stop eating highly acidic foods as well as chocolate, fatty or fried foods, coffee and carbonated drinks, you won't have it anymore. If you stop eating fatty foods, you probably won't get fatter. Headaches? Try drinking a few more glasses of water every day. Can't sleep at night? Maybe it's because you are completely stressed out or you are not getting enough physical exercise in a day. Instead of saving for liposuction to fix your appearance, all you really need to do is avoid the three-cheeseburger lunch.

You have a system to keep your health in balance and when you get sick it is your body sending you a fax that something is wrong. These days, when we get sick it's our habit to run to the doctor or the drugstore for a quick fix to our problem. We don't want to know why we're sick. We just want to be healed–now.

The whole medical field is sponsored and driven by the pharmaceutical industry. The way it wants people to get better is to take drugs. The industry is skeptical of holistic healing, or healing by love or laughter. Doctors do not look at the whole picture. They just see it through prescription glasses. It has been reported on CNN that 61 percent of American doctors receive kickbacks from the drug companies for dispensing their products. Do you think there is any motivation for doctors to sell their products? You think? I wonder about the 39 percent who didn't take the "gifts." They either have great morals or don't sell enough drugs. The drug companies have trained an entire society to take drugs for whatever ails it.

Drug companies are not interested in healing people, they are interested in selling drugs. Instead of recommending that you eat fruits and vegetables, they synthesize the good parts of the fruits and vegetables into a drug that they can sell. The reason so few nutrition studies are being done in the medical community is because the grant money goes for projects that involve the selling of millions of pills. There is no money in healthy people. It's the sick ones who pay the bills.

There are hundreds of different ways to get healthy; you just need to find the one that works for you. Depend on medication only if you absolutely have to. You have an amazing ability to heal within your own body, so take advantage of that. Millions of people have completely healed themselves through natural methods. I guess they must have imagined their way to health. And if they did, so what?

Take control of your healing. If you're having concerns about your health, by all means get them checked out as soon as pos-sible. But don't leave it completely up to the doctors or the drugs or the new procedures. Your own personal desire to get healthier is more powerful than any drug will ever be. I am in no way suggesting that you not listen to doctors. I do recommend that you get checkups often. Just don't take western medicine as the gospel to heal yourself.

You can be smarter than them anyway. If you take good care of yourself, you won't have to worry about what they say. If you are already healthy, they'll have no reason to prescribe any drugs. Make it your mission to hear great news from the doctor. "You're as healthy as a horse. You are taking great care of yourself. Nice work."

Some remedies are worse than the disease. Publius Syrus

Pursuing happiness will serve you well in your quest for good health. It is easier to act preventatively by eating good foods, taking vitamins, getting lots of fresh air, rest and exercise than it is to have heart surgery. Being healthy could be very dangerous to an illness.

When people close to you are ill, you can use your joy, love, compassion and understanding to help them heal. Being sad is a natural reaction to their misfortune. But if they're sad and you're sad, then all you have is sadness. When people are sick and dying, don't just bring flowers, bring your sparkly spirit of love and affection to the bedside. Bring little presents that will remind them how to smile. Celebrate that they're still with us, remind them how important they are to you and how much you love them. Look into their eyes, or touch your hand on their forehead and blast happy thoughts deep into their soul. There is much healing power in your smile and your gentle touch.

Keep yourself happy by being healthy. Take responsibility for being fit and feeling fine. Instead of relying on pills and gadgets to make you happy, eat good food, exercise and laugh. If you're concerned about your health, get a checkup as soon as possible. Don't let your life end early because of personal neglect. Try to keep your spirits up while you're feeling down. It will greatly improve your chances of healing as well as make your situation a lot more bearable. Your body is the vehicle that allows you to have fun. Treat it well because it's the only one you have.

MODERN BUT NOT ALWAYS EFFICIENT

My grandmother, she started walking five miles a day when she was sixty. She's ninety-seven today and we don't know where the hell she is.
Ellen Degeneres

Relax & Kick Back

I have never taken any exercise except sleeping and resting.
Mark Twain

Our society today is brimming over the top with ways to be unrelaxed. Deadlines, peer pressure, financial constraints, commuting, technology, world politics, relationships–all can stress you out like a cat caught in a dog kennel. If you find yourself getting upset more often than you would like, then maybe it's time to relax. Relaxing cleanses your soul and recharges your batteries. Relaxing is a kind of slow-paced fun. Slowing down allows your body to unwind from the stresses of your environment and the hectic pace of life. It lets you think about and reflect upon your greatest challenges. You can't escape your problems, but some solitude will help you solve them.

Do you have any relaxing moments in your life? What about the rainbows, the flowers or your friends–do you spend any time with them? When you become too stressed, your productivity goes down, your anxiety goes up and life seems disastrous. Even though it may seem as if you're unable to take the time off, you will probably find that relaxing for even just a few minutes will leave you mentally refreshed and will do wonders for your ability to face the day. Making the time at the right time is the biggest challenge. Don't blow up the tractor trying to harvest the entire crop.

Far away from the horns, exhaust and busyness of the city you will find the natural world. You were born a part of nature, then you cut yourself away from it with your own hand. Being connected to the earth and all of its creatures is important. You can feel the stress dissipate as you step into the organic world. It could be as simple as watching a good rainstorm stroll across the horizon, ducks feeding at the park, a majestic waterfall or a dancing fire. Good visuals give good vibes.

A ruffled mind makes a restless pillow. Charlotte Bronte

Enjoy listening to croaking frogs or crickets on a hot summer's night. When I get stressed, I grab the tent and head for the bush. I just sit around contemplating life while watching the birds fight over a few berries. The sound of the crashing waves or even the wind whispering past my cranium is sheer delight. How do you feel after sitting on the beach in the warm sun? What about after a walk in the woods? How do you feel after commuting through rush-hour traffic?

Most people have trouble unwinding because they have become too wound up in the first place. You become like a stress piggy bank–every stressful moment is stored inside you. When you finally go on vacation, it takes a week to empty the bank of all the stress inside. Don't let it get too full in the first place. Too much activity blocks the insights one can gain in quiet moments. Without relaxation, you can expect health problems and a lack of grins.

What do you think they invented Sundays for anyway? Quiet time helps to eliminate the negative distractions in your life. If you are feeling pain or encountering phenomenal challenges, take some time to reflect. When you are encompassed by dark shadows, you need to seek out some R&R.

Quiet time is almost the same thing as relaxing, but it's just a little different. Relaxing can be a day or two or three or even a week, whereas quiet time is usually only a few minutes or a few hours. Quiet time is the mini recharge that can be utilized by anybody. Every person needs that time where they don't have to answer to anyone. It's like building an imaginary fortress around you. Even just a couple of minutes will give you the chance to think through your current challenges or refresh your spirit.

The deluxe version of quiet time is the act of napping. Napping is nature's pit stop. Many grownups feel that naps are a form of weakness. I think they are a form of recharge, a mini gift to yourself for getting tired in the first place. Unplug the phone, get your favorite blanket and catch some afternoon z's. Numerous countries around the world practice the afternoon siesta, so why not you? If your body says take a nap, why resist? What would happen if you didn't listen to your body when it said, "I have to pee now"?

Discover what stresses you out, then stop doing it. Then identify the activities that unstress you and practice them on a regular basis. Try prayer, meditation, massages and bubble baths. Sit in the sun, sit in the shade and let your stress leave. Take a nap or take a mental health day. Let the gods of relaxation come into your circulation system and distribute tiny little grins to each and every one of your cells. I encourage living life to the fullest but never to the point of becoming obsessed with achieving, seeing and doing everything. Get a little unserious about your life and just relax.

Now and then it's good to pause in our pursuit of happiness and just be happy.
Guillame Apollinaire

Relationships & Sex

Smile; it's the second best thing one can do with one's lips. Unknown

When I talk about relationships, I'm talking about your main squeeze. The person you play naked games with. How is your relationship with him or her? Is it OK, is it fantastic or is it awful? Do you have a major relationship in your life right now? If not, we'll get to that in a minute. If you do, let's chat.

I believe that a positive intimate relationship with someone is the greatest gift you can experience during your lifetime. Incredible waves of love, spiritual connection and general good vibrations are all side effects of a positive relationship. There is something very magical about two people coming together and making a bigger spiritual entity.

A relationship should be built on honesty and complete trust. Other words that come to mind are respect, support and unconditional acceptance. Happy relationships seem to have a sense of responsibility and commitment. The players are more focused on what they can give instead of what they can get. Successful relationships have excellent communication, and listening is practiced on a regular basis. So, what does this have to do with fun?

If you're involved with a miserable bitch/bastard, you will never be able to have fun to your fullest potential. You are a lot better off by yourself than you are with an abusive or insensitive partner. Some people are just attached to unloneliness and will put up with an awful lot of shit to stay that way. If you compromise in this department, you cut yourself off from the person or persons that could make a wonderful addition to your life.

Relationships will have ups and downs; the tide goes in and the tide goes out. It is silly to think that you will have a perfect relationship because they rarely, if ever, exist. From a spiritual sense, I believe we are brought together in relationships to grow as a team and as individuals. When that learning ends, it is time to move on with the knowledge you have and set off into the world. If there is any kind of physical, emotional or mental abuse in a relationship, it may cross the line between being beneficial and being detrimental to happiness.

COMMUNICATION

So there are many ebbs and flows to a relationship. Just because people make a great couple doesn't guarantee a good union. It's perfectly normal not to be head over heels in love twenty-four hours a day, seven days a week. Sometimes you have to evaluate where you're at and where you want to go. Nothing is constant in this world. We are all changing every day. Sometimes your physical closeness will disappear, but your spiritual connection can continue to deepen. In life, generally we enjoy different things at different stages and it's the same with the different stages of relationships.

If you have different primary goals in life, then it may be time for you to go your separate ways. Through communication, you can discover what is important to you and your partner. So many people think that because you've been together for a long time your partner should know you, and if they don't they're somehow bad. People can be telepathic, but you should never expect your partner to automatically know what is going on with you. If you are secretive and covert about what is bothering you, it is only going to fester into a giant spider's nest. It will take merely a toothpick to bust it open and nasty spiders will be everywhere.

A NASTY SPIDER

Avoid blaming the other person for your problems and expecting them to make it all better.

If you haven't communicated what's troubling you, how can they ever please you? When couples fall in love, they tend to overlook the potentials for disagreements while they're in the romance trance. Then when the dust settles and all the sparks are gone, all they have is each other.

Never use excuses to avoid what is really happening with your significant other. He only lies to me once in a while. She can't control her anger and that's why she hits me. He only drinks so that he can feel better. She said this was the last time she would sleep with the whole hockey team while I'm babysitting. How long would you be friends with someone if they lied to you all the time? What if they punched you in the head every so often? Relationships are about two people growing together. They are not about one person abusing the crap out of the other.

If you're single, you're in a far better position than someone who is getting abused. Whatever stage your relationship is at, I encourage you to evaluate to see if you are happy or not. If it is worth saving, go see a counselor or get some books on solving your problems. If there are kids involved, it is a difficult situation. Staying together may help your children but if you are experiencing misery, it will only make it worse for them. Love and relationships are never easy and when there are little munchkins involved it only becomes more intricate. Good luck and I wish you the best.

If you need to, pack a suitcase and get the hell out. If you're hanging out with someone who really doesn't do much for you, you are repelling the person who could. It takes a lot less effort to leave than it does to take crap from people.

If you've just been dumped, celebrate that you can now find someone who appreciates you. If you've been the dumper, you have done that person a favor; they can now find someone who truly appreciates them. You deserve a pat on the back for having the courage to remove yourself from a situation that wasn't good for either of you. Life is too short to be in a relationship that is not growing in love, compassion, understanding and tolerance.

Somewhere in the world there is a person who will truly appreciate you and everything about you. There are more than six billion people on the planet and half of them are of your favorite gender. When you narrow it down to your age group and the ones that are available, you still have a gene pool of about one hundred million people. Maybe you'll never find the one for you, but why give up trying when your odds are so good? There are plenty of trees in the forest.

Past relationships can have effects on our confidence and self-esteem. We tend to lump our last lover in with all our potential lovers. Since she was a beautiful person and she ended up hating me, then all beautiful people hate me. Or, "Every time I open my heart to someone, they rip it out and do a little Riverdance on it." Or the regular line of excuses: I am too old, ugly or smelly to ever get somebody. If you spend all your time moping around because of a bad or former relationship, it just shows that your former lover was right about you.

I can remember when the air was clean and sex was dirty. George Burns

Do you like somebody? Then pursue it. Make that first call. If they don't want to luxuriate in your wonders, then keep looking. It begins with never taking it personally. It is not that they don't like you, they're just perceptually challenged in discovering what a fantastic person you are. Be proud of your uniqueness and keep getting out into the marketplace. You say, "I'm tired of the bar scene." Well, duh ... stop going to the bar. Sign up for a dating service, search the Web, join an activity club, go to the beach, go on vacation–do whatever you love and there you'll find others who have the same interests you do. Pursuing a life of fun and having a fun mentality will help you attract another pleasurable lover, and if it doesn't at least you're having a good time.

When you go out on a date, try to keep your expectations to a minimum. Just because you are going for a date doesn't mean you have to marry this person. Instead of compulsively trying to find Mr. or Mrs. Right, just go have some fun. Avoid evaluating people in the first few seconds. When you wait for the "perfect" lover, you lose out on the possibility of intimate moments, giggles, laughs and orgasms.

Enjoy the process of meeting new people. You don't need to go through your mental checklist to see if they have every single quality. People take dating so seriously. All you're doing is shopping for a human you want to spend time with. What's the big hairy deal? Lighten up. If you can enjoy the process, at least you can have some fun while you're searching. I would rather be refused a thousand times than never love at all. So just go enjoy the fact that someone went out with you in the first place.

Be open minded; it could happen any time. Finding a lover is strictly a numbers game. Don't take it personal when you are refused; just move on. Babe Ruth was a great batter, but he was even better at striking out. Have a positive expectation that you will find someone who is both deserving and ready for the gifts you have to share.

Maybe you have some preconceived notions about what people are like in general. All men are pigs or all women like to play games. Everybody is different, and if you lump them all into one group, you are setting yourself up for misery and loneliness.

I don't care how much you believe there may not be somebody compatible for you. I have seen people go single for twenty, thirty or forty years only to find the absolutely perfect person. It doesn't matter how long you've been looking as long as you're still looking. If you give up, you will have nothing. If you pursue your desire to have a mate one day, you will find someone.

Through all of my school years and my early adult life, I was a total loser when it came to women. By the time I was twenty-six I had never had a girlfriend for longer than a month. This made me very lonely and horny. I committed to figure out why. Was I ugly? Was I smelly? Was I gay? I had to figure out why I wasn't being loved by the ladies. I worked on it for a whole summer, taking seminars, reading books, kissing watermelons and working on myself.

My biggest problem was that I felt intimidated by beautiful women. I was terrified that I would screw up and somehow not be able to impress them with an image of who I thought I was. Consequently I was trying too hard, made myself too available and gave them no challenge. I had to get grounded, get a better sense of who I was and remain confident without worrying about how they would perceive me. Once I realized I was OK just the way I was, I began to have a choice of women. I remember coming home to find six messages on my answering machine from women who wanted to take me out. I can tell you that from my loser beginnings to my satisfied adult life, the payoff is a thousand times the effort.

Look at your singleness as a time for personal growth. Spend the time and effort to get in shape physically, mentally, financially and emotionally. You will multiply your chances of finding a lover and you will most certainly improve the quality of your life. When you are done, get out into the marketplace.

While you are out looking for a lover, you may discover better ways to live, a bounty of new experiences and you may even make a new friend or two. If you manage to get a pony ride–congratulations. If you manage to find your sweetheart, then well done. You have more potential for pleasure then you could ever imagine.

Let's say you do get involved in a great relationship and everything is peachy. How can you fun up your relationship? Most of these concepts that relate to a fun life also relate to having a fun relationship. Begin by getting rid of the Mind Poo. Communicate with each other so that if things are bothering you, you can bring them out into the open where they can be discussed in a civil manner. Never use guilt, no matter how tempting it can be.

Add playfulness, spontaneity, creativity, silliness, laughing and friendship. Communicate your expectations so that you each know where you are coming from. Instead of judging, try unconditional acceptance. Avoid trying to change your lover because chances are you will only be resented. The most important thing you can do for a healthy relationship is appreciate your lover for exactly who they are. Not what you wish they could be but for what is sitting in front of you. Focus on what is really great about them, not what is wrong with them.

When I'm good, I'm very good, but when I'm bad, I'm better. Mae West

When you are in love, you make certain aspects of your lover very bright and bigger than they are. When things aren't going so well, we tend to see leaving the cap off the toothpaste as a devastating character flaw. Does your partner make you feel good most or all of the time, or do they just provide some sex and pay half the rent? If you are not getting along, find out why. It is worth putting a little effort into something so rewarding as a loving relationship.

Speaking of sex–oooh, sex is fun. When two lovers come together to get jiggy with it, it is an amazing experience. Describing a good sexual experience is difficult to put into words, but our culture has more hang-ups about sex and nudity than I can put in a single book.

When you were young, your curiosity about sex was quickly extinguished by whatever means possible. Guilt and feelings of shame were dolloped upon us when we were just trying to figure out what our special organs were for. If you were caught thinking about it, you would be punished and ridiculed. What's so bad about sex anyway? It's a natural primal urge that needs to be expressed and satisfied. There's nothing wrong with copious amounts of warm fuzzy feelings and plenty of orgasms.

Now sex is a very personal thing and every person has a different opinion of what is right and what is wrong. It is not something that should be treated frivolously. Live by your own morals. Don't let society or religion or anybody dictate your sexual behavior. You know what is right and what is wrong. Rape is terrible and messing with children is despicable, but there's nothing wrong with acting out the odd naughty fantasy.

I really don't believe that when the creator created our sexual bits he was also writing a giant rule book on the exact way it should be performed. Whatever you do in the privacy of your own home with consenting adults is your business, so operate sexually the way that feels good for you. Sex does not have to be serious all the time. Have sex in the middle of a rainstorm, invite some friends over (ensure there are some sandwiches on hand), make

a day of it. Overhaul a prudish attitude and experiment with new sexual techniques. Get creative, get some toys, get some lotions, get some Jell-O, chocolate or whipped cream. Go ahead, add some fun and giggles to the bedroom.

Let your partner know exactly what tickles your fancy. Understand what steps need to be taken to titillate your lover. Then keep titillating. When you're having deep personal moments, enjoy their touch on your skin or the way your toes curl. Feel the breath of your lover–enjoy every single curve and cell of his or her body. If you are having a sexual relationship with someone, cherish it like a beautiful sunrise. Love your nakedness. Love your body. Love your lover and never ever feel ashamed of your sexuality.

Sometimes you may want to help yourself to happiness. In the 1700s it was believed that masturbation was a sickness, but it just isn't true. Masturbation is totally natural and easily executed. Scientific studies show you can't go blind or grow hair on the palms of your hands. God gave us these pleasure tools, so you may as well enjoy them.

If you're out there swinging your strudel or walking the poodle, make sure you use a condom. Getting or giving sexually transmitted diseases or AIDS is not fun and is, in fact, really stupid. Sex is designed to be life-enhancing, not debilitating. Have fun with sex, have safe sex and leave the critics behind. Discover the delights of naughtiness.

When you do have someone special, appreciate every little morsel of them. Become adventurous with sex as long as it's right for you. Either fix or get out of bad relationships as fast as you can. If you are single, embrace it and find a way to enjoy it. Use your singleness as an opportunity to improve on yourself. Dating does not have to be a big deal; just enjoy the process. Seek out intimacy and special relationships whenever you can.

Love is life. And if you miss love you miss life. Leo Buscaglia

Just Say No

The art of leadership is saying no, not yes.
It's very easy to say yes. Tony Blair

A lot of times we have trouble saying no. People use guilt and fear to motivate us to fit into their plans. Most people tend to spend their time saying yes to events they don't enjoy and no to the things they do like. It's easy to form a habit of saying yes to whomever asks favors of you. However, a much more powerful habit is to say no to them and yes to yourself.

When you say no, you give yourself power by living by your rules. It's your life and you have no time for unwanted tasks. As much as you want to make people happy, you can't please everybody no matter how hard you try. I'm not suggesting you be rude to people to have things your way. Just don't agree to do things you hate.

Don't let unpleasant chores bog you down. Either pay people to do them or avoid them altogether. If your schedule is filled with unwanted obligations, fun cannot come your way because you're spending all your time working towards miserableness.

For me, the most unpleasant task I can think of is moving. I hate moving. I despise it; just the thought of it sends shudders down my spine. The only thing I hate more than moving is helping other people move. I can never understand why anybody would want to burden the ones they love with such a chore. When I move, I pay movers; when my friends move, I wish them well.

If you are invited to a dinner party and you don't want to go, what do you do? Your hosts are always prattling on about how much trouble they've gone to to please you. "We've been baking for three weeks. We've been expecting you. You have to come." But every time you go there, it turns into a bitch session about life and the couple love to fight with each other. If you would rather just stay home and read a book, then do. Just when you feel that the vortex of guilt and manipulation is sucking you in, say NO.

When you say yes to an event you don't want to attend, you are disrespecting yourself and your hosts. To be present in flesh only and not in spirit is an insult to you and whomever asked you to be there. A kindly "no thank you" is a blessing to all parties involved. If you find yourself saying, "I would rather stick chopsticks up my nose than go to their place for dinner," it's time for you to say no.

Politely refuse activities you have no time for or interest in. Say no to phone solicitors, high-pressure salespeople and buying impulses. Say no to fatty food and say yes to your health. Say no to polluting companies and unfair business practices. Say no to a stinky job or a stinky relationship. Say no to people or activities that foster Mind Poo. Do not let your mind be poisoned by chronic anger, fear or sadness. Say yes to your peace of mind. Say no to acting out in rage or cowering in fear. Be motivated by power and choice, not by fear, guilt or imagined obligation.

Learning to say no to the negative influences of the news will help multiply your feelings of happiness. For so many people the day starts with news on the radio or reading the newspaper. And what can we learn there? A family is killed by drug dealers, a kitty has been found in a microwave oven, and the daily death count from the highways. Then there are the plane crashes, drug busts and child abductions. Moving along, there is the section on lying politicians and war criminals. After that you can read about the Middle East and their inability to be friends. Watching television news is like watching a horror show except there are no actors–only real people suffering and dying.

You can argue until you're blue in the face about how important that information is, but how does it affect you on a day-to-day basis? How will your ability to worry change this situation? It can't. Why in the world do I need to know about microwaved kitty? Perhaps when I go to work we can all feel really shitty talking about easy-bake kitty at the first coffee break. You do not need to live the tragedies of the world over and over again.

My life doesn't really depend on knowing if a house fire killed a family of six, or if the government in some faraway country is corrupt. Somewhere along the path we have been told that the sky is not only falling but is an even more dangerously falling sky than first reported! We are conditioned to hear, watch or read the "bad" news sometimes twice, three, four times a day. Why permit other people to enter the sacred mansion of your mind to deposit their dilemmas, misery and lies?

There was a time in history when the troubles of society were not slapped in people's faces. They were still able to breathe, eat and sleep and have happy lives. My god, no wonder we have trouble being happy when every single day we are handed a report on exactly how much misery took place in the world in the last twenty-four hours.

The media gives a selective, distorted, sensationalized version of our world. You have the ability to close the door and keep it out. If you really need to know the big news, believe me, there are more than enough news followers happy to tell you all the latest propa-ganda. If you just need sports scores, business news or weather information, selectively find what you want and avoid the death and misery.

Saying no to television is saying yes to activities in your life that you really enjoy. But so many people spend so much time in front of a television, it must be the greatest form of fun around, right? Let's look at the benefits of watching television.

- It helps you to become a mindless drone
- Keeps your violent-image tank filled to the brim
- Keeps you up-to-date with the world death count
- Keeps you away from activities that make you smile too much
- Allows you to watch people who have lives so that don't need your own
- Lets you accumulate useless knowledge that may help you in a game of Trivial Pursuit

Television is like the American toaster, you push the button and the same thing pops up every time. Alfred Hitchcock

Television is a boring, non-interactive way to entertain yourself. You may be amused and entertained, but you will never face your fears, feel an adrenaline rush or have a life-changing encounter. There is an opportunity to learn and be inspired, but if you never leave the couch, what's the point? When it comes to a fun life, television is the butt steak of beef, the Lada of limos, the beans and wieners of gourmet cooking.

Television is the bland leading the bland. Murray Schumach

The average American watches TV four hours a day. That's 1,500 hours a year. Compare this to the fact that a year in school is 900 classroom hours.

What else could you do in 1,500 hours? Get a university education, help out in the community or become excellent at any sport or activity. By the age of sixteen, the average American teenager will have witnessed 200,000 acts of TV violence, 33,000 of which are murders. It is hard to find a show that doesn't have guns, adultery, deceit or criminal behavior. I am not a bible thumper, but this can't be of any benefit to you. What if you had or participated in 200,000 giggles and 33,000 belly laughs instead?

The more TV you are watching, the fewer enjoyable life experiences you are having. There are so many things we could do that would be better for us. But we still keep being drawn to it as if it were a giant magnet. We will sit for hours watching nothing, learning nothing and becoming nothing. Yes, there are some quality television programs out there, but they are so few and far between that it's not really worth it.

Another side effect of watching too much television is that when you have a conversation with another human, it's about what you saw on TV last night. There is no need to talk about your dreams and desires because you can talk about the dreams and desires of all the fantasy people on TV. And when you're not doing that, you're comparing your life to these make-believe characters and becoming depressed because of your pitiful existence.

Think about it. You are comparing yourself to people who have their dialogue written for them. They are dressed and made up by other people, then they pretend to be someone they aren't. Is that really who you want to idolize? We look at television as real and our lives as unreal. Turn off the TV before you spend another moment trying to enjoy somebody else's life when you really should be enjoying your own.

Look at adventure based reality shows. It is all about people challenging themselves to be more and have adventurous experiences. Why would you ever want to watch someone else have fun? It's like watching naked people movies; it is certainly nowhere close to the real experience. But on the bright side, thank God there are still people with lives who will climb the mountains and play in life. If there weren't, all the shows on television would be adventure shows about other people watching TV.

Some people may argue that it's a great escape from the day's troubles, or that it keeps us informed. But what if you took all the hours that you watch television and used them for something you truly enjoy? Master a musical instrument, volunteer in the community or tend to your garden. There are probably a thousand different life enriching ways of spending your time. Fun, active people watch very little if any TV.

The same argument goes for video games. If you enjoy them, great, but if you're playing them all the time, then look out. Video games turn children into mindless drones with excellent eye-thumb coordination and stressed vision. Children should be out playing baseball or basketball or discovering nature. Video addicts have poor social skills, poor fitness levels and limited curiosity. With all the electronic entertainment available today, family activities seem to be almost a thing of the past.

Television has proved that people will look at anything rather than each other.
Ann Landers

If you dare, cut off your cable, turn off the TV and strange things will start to happen. You may have an in-depth conversation with your friends. Instead of letting the gamma rays eat the cells in your brain, you will probably start going for walks and inventing new games to play. Why watch sex on television when you could be experiencing it first-hand (no pun intended)? Become aware of how much time you're spending watching TV and playing video games. Make a conscious decision to cut down or stop it all together.

Television is not the only place where Mind Poo is rampant; the movie industry is rife with it too. Hollywood tells us that it reflects our society and encourages the viewer to think about the way it really is. They must have bought a lousy mirror because in all my years I have never actually seen a murder, a rape or a gun being shot. It is not a reflection of day-to-day life. There is more to life than cold-blooded murder, cool cops and violence. Ask yourself, "Does the material that I am reading, watching or listening to make me a better person?"

When it comes to the world in general, you can say no to companies or businesses that you do not agree with. If a company is breaking environmental laws or human rights laws or is selling a deadly product–do not support it. If you have been treated poorly by a business, write a letter of complaint. Say no to keeping quiet and say yes to expressing how you feel. It may not make a difference to the business's bottom line, but it certainly can make a difference to yours.

Las Vegas wasn't built in a day and it will take a little practice, but once you begin to choose fun over crap, life becomes easier and easier. Being assertive and saying no to unwanted experiences gives you the power and self-esteem to help you achieve supreme funness. Insist on being treated with respect as a person, but do not infringe on the rights of others to get it. Use your no's wisely and say yes to yourself wherever and whenever you can.

Fun at Home

A comfortable house is a great source of happiness.
Sydney Smith.

The world may be unsure and unsafe, but your home is the one place that you need to feel relaxed and comfortable. And a number of things can affect your home happiness level. The first question to ask yourself is, "Am I living where I want to live?"

Do you want to live in the desert or would you rather wet your tongue residing by the water? How's the neighborhood? Do you feel safe? Or do your neighbors upset you off on a regular basis? Do you hate living in the city? Does the local weather get you down? Do you spend all your time just trying to keep your house clean? Does it take two hours of your life to commute every day? Sure, moving is a hassle, but living where you don't want to be is depressing.

If you really aren't happy, start thinking about where you really want to live. I don't think it's healthy to live in the same house for most of your life. In prehistoric times, people would move according to the seasons. In our time we have the option to live just about anywhere we decide. Just because your family has lived in your house or your town for 212 years doesn't mean you have to. Yes, it can be a big deal to move across the country, but if it doesn't work out, you can always move back.

The first time I came to Vancouver, I remember sitting at a bus stop and listening to a street musician belting out the blues on a harmonica. I fell in love and vowed to live here. It was very difficult in the beginning, but I was determined to stay. For five months, I slept on a couch and ate twenty-five-cent Oriental noodles to survive. If you want something better in your life, you will have to make sacrifices. And I am sure glad I did. In the spring, I can ski in the morning and go to the beach in the afternoon. How many cities in the world are there where you can do that?

So let's say you're happy with your location. What do you need to change around the house to make it more pleasurable for you? Do you need some brighter colors? Do you need to take out a wall or build a deck? Can you sit on the floor without feeling you're breaking a rule? Do you want a hammock in your living room? What about a climbing wall in the basement? If you want to put your couch in the kitchen and race toy cars in the garage, go right ahead. If you want to paint your walls electric pink, whatever. It's your home, so make it a place of joy. Spark your imagination and think outside the box to make your house the most pleasurable for you.

A nice house may show how much money you have. But a nice home also shows how much spirit you have. Is your home warm, welcoming and fun or is it serious and sterile? How much giggling have you heard in your home lately? Make it OK for people to thoroughly enjoy themselves in your home. If there are any negative influences, get them out. I used to have a very close friend who would only come over to bitch about his life. I laid down the law and reminded him that my house is a sacred place and if he wanted to dump miserableness, this bank was not accepting deposits. Yes, your friends or family may need to unload their problems every once in a while, but any more than that and they need to be gagged and left out back. Make your home a "No Mind Poo" zone.

Every fun person I have ever met has something quirky in their house that makes them smile. Put up inspirational photos and silly wall hangings. You don't have to turn your house into a circus tent, but you can put up a few things that warm your heart. Bring a lighthearted approach to your home and you will be amazed at the results. If you need to change something structurally in your house to make it more comfortable, don't worry about the resale value. Think of the smile value.

Have nothing in your house that you do not know to be useful or believe to be beautiful. William Morris

Your home is your sanctuary, your safe place and the fortress where you keep your stuff. Are you cluttering up your life with material things? Avoid status items and focus on comfort items. What if you have so many things you can't appreciate them all. Does your stuff tie you down? Are you scared to go away for the weekend because somebody might come and steal all your fantastic stuff? Then your stuff is dictating your activity schedule.

Every item in your house should serve some kind of purpose. If its only purpose is to take up space, then it will take some of your psychological space as well. Go through every closet and every corner where there is a pile o' crap party going on. Clean your refrigerator, the dresser, the bathroom or the garage. If there are bad vibes attached to something you own, why keep it? Like gifts from people you no longer get along with. Or presents you've accepted that are so ugly they make you retch every time you look at them. Have a garage sale, give your excess stuff to charity. Do whatever you need to get rid of the useless material possessions. Someone else can now enjoy the stuff that was cluttering your life.

Now what about your clothes? Are they comfortable? Are they quality or are you embarrassed to wear them? It's much better to have a few nice things than a closet full of rags. Or perhaps you're a fashion hound, always buying the very latest designs even if they don't suit you or are about as comfortable as a straitjacket. Buy your stuff because it feels good and fits your needs, not because your gaggle of material possessions impresses the Joneses.

Do you like the art, furniture, pots, pans, dishes or entertainment equipment you own? Do the eggs stick to the pan every time you use it? Have you always wanted a thick

fluffy comforter? Do you have a comfortable bed? You say you can't afford all these new things? Well, then appreciate what you have, get rid of what you can and we'll talk about money in the next two chapters.

Did you ever see an unhappy horse? Did you ever see a bird that had the blues?
One reason why birds and horses are not unhappy is because
they are not trying to impress other birds and horses. Dale Carnegie

HAVING TOO MUCH STUFF

Some people have lots of fine things in their home–fine china, silverware and furniture. Do you use it? Or is the plastic still on the couches? Does your house feel like a china shop? If you touch anything, you may be hauled away by security? Don't sit on the floor, don't speak too loudly and certainly never dance around the lamps. If you have nice things, then use them. Bring out the good dishes and sit on the good furniture. Make every day a special occasion. Why buy something that you use only one or two days a year?

As far as the occupants of your house go–are you fighting with your spouse, aggravated by your kids or disrespected by your roommate? There is only one thing to do. Learn how to communicate gently with the people you live with. Clear up disputes about chores, messiness, noise and space. Clearly define what the house rules are. If you can understand each other and work together, you will create opportunities for joy. Better communication will form strong bonds and mutual respect. You should never speak loudly to each other unless there is a fire.

Instead of every person for themselves, the participants will feel they're part of something bigger. When I was in New Zealand, I met a family of five who had just spent the last two years living on a sailboat. Because they were on a sailboat isolated out on the water, everyone had to work as a team. The three kids, who were ten, eight and six, were amazing friends, remarkably mature and well-mannered for their age. Mom and Dad's dedication to building a family team made everyone stronger as individuals.

What can you do as a team? Clean the house as a team, play as a team and confront challenges as a team. Don't dump all the chores on one person, then sit around waiting for them to finish. Work together and then when it is all done, go have some fun. The family that plays together stays together. Instead of always choosing individual forms of entertainment, look for activities you can do as a group. When planning fun activities as a family, make sure everybody has input. Of course, every member will want to do their own thing on their own time and this needs to be respected. Look for similarities in your pleasures, not your differences.

A SAMPLE FAMILY ACTIVITY

Having a family is like having a bowling alley installed in your brain.
Martin Mull

For a lot of people, everything changes when children pop out of the womb. Obviously your life will change and your priorities will be askew. Your entire life can be turned upside down with sleep deprivation and constant giving of attention. Keep this in mind. With children you will have different things that bring you joy, but never forget that you need to have your own personal fun. Yes, give to your children, but give to yourself as well. Just creatively work it into your schedule and you will be a better person to your kids and your spouse. Otherwise you will just be resentful, wondering what is missing out of your life.

Don't you think that two heads are not better than one, if both are stupid? Unknown

If your family or relatives are a bunch of peanutheads, then you just have to accept them as they are. You can't change your relatives, but you can control how much they influence your life. If you're turning yourself into a basketful of needless misery because of your situation at home, you need to make some changes. Talk to the team and work things out. If your roommate is an asshole, maybe it's time for one of you to move. It's not selfish to demand that your home be the one place where you should feel happy, safe and comfortable.

Happy up your home and sooner or later it's going to happy up the neighborhood. Say hello to people, help them when they need it. I used to live on James Street in Vancouver. Every year over the Labour Day weekend the street was closed and turned into a giant party. Vancouver is a very multicultural city, so when the potluck lunch came out, numerous countries were represented. People came with violins and guitars and filled the streets with music. We played street hockey with children of all ages and munched on tasty worldly delights. It was the best part of living on James Street.

Get to know your neighbors and you will build a sense of trust, which builds communities. You can have an abundance of friends as well as plenty of allies looking out for crime, keeping the kids safe and contributing to keeping your home a happy place. What could you do to happy up your neighborhood?

Challenge your choice of where you live, clean out the clutter and the bad bits. Get rid of the whiners, play with your family, respect each other and enjoy yourself. Discover new activities that bring your family or roommates towards happiness. Having a safe, comfortable home should always be a priority for you.

Beer is proof that God loves us and wants us to be happy.
Ben Franklin

Fun at Work

I love my job, it's the work I hate. Winston Churchill

You spend most of your waking day either at work, getting to and from work or thinking about work. You might as well enjoy yourself. People rarely have success in work or business unless they have fun doing it. There are two ways to have fun at work. Find a job you enjoy or take pleasure in the job you have. When you work at a job you hate, you have to ask yourself, "Why am I here?"

Workers in America consume fifteen tons of aspirin a day, so it's not a big surprise to find out that not every single person on the planet is working at his or her dream job. You may be learning certain skills, preparing for another career or just paying the bills. Some people are just killing time. Killing time is a very difficult activity.

Why do you do what you do? What part of your soul is being fulfilled? Does your work help you grow as a person? Does your job enhance your self-esteem and pride? You must evaluate your work to see if it's right for you. Most people spend forty hours a week at their job. Forty hours a week for forty years is 800,000 hours or about 10,000 workdays. If you work 10,000 days at a job you don't like, doesn't that sound more like a jail sentence than a career? Sure the benefits are good, like medical and dental, but if your job is giving you stress and causing your teeth to fall out, the benefits really aren't that great, are they? Is this what you want to do with your days, or would you rather be somewhere else?

Work isn't so much about having fun as it is about receiving satisfaction from what you do. You receive joy from your work because it is challenging or fulfilling. You must do work that you are proud of or care about, or what is the point of being there? It is wonderful to feel that afterglow of satisfaction after completing a difficult task that demanded our best.

Maybe you spend too much time at work. Do you really have to work 60 or 70 hours a week? Do you work six days when you could work five? Could you work four? Why are you a workaholic? Are you avoiding some other issue by working all the time? If you absolutely love your job, then all the power to you. If you don't like your job and you're a workaholic, what you really need is a slap upside the head.

You may have been pressured by family members to follow a certain career path. Maybe it was the money, the prestige or the fame. Maybe you didn't think there were any other options. There could have been a time when you really enjoyed what you were doing, but now it's not as enjoyable as it once was. You spend so much time at work. Don't you think you should thoroughly enjoy yourself?

When the alarm clock rings, do you say yahoo or boo-hoo? Your job should make your heart go pitter-patter with excitement, not stress. Does your job have meaning? Whose life do you make better? What matters most to you, a big fat paycheck, or a big fat smile on your face? Work is good, but your happiness is much more important. You may have a fantastic job, but the commute and the workload make you unavailable and therefore negatively affects people who are close to you.

What about your environment? Do you have fresh air or is it pumped in through miles of ventilation? Is there sunshine or those annoying fluorescent lights? Is it relaxing or is it intense? If you don't like your environment or your co-workers, then it's time to move on. If idiots surround you and your boss is an idiot, what does that make you? When you're trapped at a job you don't like, you will become a permanent victim of weasel wretchedness.

If you don't get a kick out of the job you are doing you'd better hunt another one. Samuel Vauclain

Hundreds of thousands of different careers are available to you. Somewhere in the world there is a place where your efforts will be truly appreciated. If you had enough money to live without working, what would you do? That's the ideal career for you.

It begins with a dream. If you can see it happening in your head, it can happen in reality. What job would give you the most satisfaction? You may not be able to quit your smelly job at this time, but you can work toward your goal of a career change as you go. If you do one thing every single day towards a new career, no matter how small it is, sooner rather than later you will have your new job.

Start thinking about where you want to go. Then figure out how you are going to get there. If you want something more, it will take more effort. You may have to give up your weekends or take night classes. You may have to spend time hitting the books. But a year or two of sweat and toil towards something that can give you immense satisfaction is a drop in the bucket compared to 10,000, 5,000 or even 1,000 days at a job that sucks. If you aren't happy with your job, you may as well get ready for the job that will make you happy.

Now, if changing jobs is not an immediate option, consider making your job more fun. No matter what you do, there isn't a job out there that couldn't benefit from a lighthearted approach. For some of us, though, it can be very hard to have fun at work because we perceive that somehow this will stop, slow or destroy our ability to perform. It is a huge benefit to your employer when you enjoy your job; otherwise you will bring down all the people around you.

Corporate America is realizing that a happy employee is a productive employee. Employees who have fun together build up an abundance of good feelings towards one another. When things get tough or stressful, the good times shared together help balance out the bad. Happy employees get sick less often, have fewer disputes with co-workers and work their butts off to get things done. You can make your workplace more fun without sacrificing professionalism. Having fun and working are not opposites.

Getting fired is nature's way to telling you that you had the wrong job in the first place. Hal Lancaster

There are plenty of little things that can open up the door to a more enjoyable work environment. Take pride in what you do. It's not what you do that counts; it's how you feel about it. Whatever your job is, do it well and feel satisfied. You have nothing to lose and everything to gain. With all the layoffs and firings nowadays, you need to keep your sense of humor more than ever.

How can we be more playful at work? Start by bringing a good attitude to work. Feel free to laugh. Create games out of your work chores. Use your break time for whatever you want–napping, a walk or meeting a secret lover. Attach cartoons to boring memos or a tissue to sad ones. Avoid office politics and gossip; they suck your time, energy and credibility. Surround yourself with stimuli like pictures of mentors, happy photos or toys. Delete the negative and enhance the positive. There are plenty of books available on fun techniques and companies that use fun as a tool for their success.

T.H. Jones
Sales Manager

Fun at work usually begins at the top. The management or owner will generally dictate the amount of giggles allowed in the workplace. If the management has brains made out of turnips, you still have options. Avoid clock watching. Wear comfortable clothes. Yes, brothers and sisters, get rid of those high heels. Watch what you eat and drink at work. Coffee, sweets and heavy lunches combined with a general lack of sleep can magnify your misery. Learn to enjoy working with others and encourage them to enjoy working with you.

Use your imagination and professionalism to encourage an environment of enjoyment. If you can make your work your play and your play your work, you win. If you don't like your job, then move on. There is a buffet of career opportunities available. If you are presently unemployed, feel free to rejoice. Use this time to improve and expand your marketable skills.

If you're too tied down to move on, here are some more options. Work one day a week at a place that you absolutely love. Maybe it's a daycare, a ski hill or a campground. Start to discover new possibilities without having to throw your life into financial turmoil by walking away from your job.

You could start a small business cutting lawns, selling hot dogs from a cart or selling Tupperware. Could you start a business that lets people have fun? Could you give hiking or biking tours, for example? There are great tax benefits to starting a small business and, who knows, you might be so good at it you can quit your stinking job. You will never know till you try. It gives you something you can call your own. If you are going to start a small business, do something that you really enjoy. If you don't enjoy it, all you're doing is extending your workweek.

Throughout my life, I have met many people with outrageous jobs: being the guardian to the Stanley Cup, beer testers, golf club testers, professional partiers and more. I have worked as a radio station traffic reporter who worked from a bicycle, a Frisbee instructor and a travel photographer. Whatever it is, there are good times and a paycheck waiting for you. Believe that it is possible, believe that you deserve it and you will find a more satisfying career. If you want a more fun job, there are thousands and thousands of fun jobs out there and they all need to be filled by people who are enthusiastic about them. Network every opportunity you get and be prepared to reinvent yourself so your dream occupation can happen.

I never worked a day in my life. It's not work when you love what you're doing. David Shakarian

There are millions of fun jobs in the world. Just because your parents had miserable jobs doesn't mean you have to. Search out people who are being paid for the things you enjoy. You will quickly realize that they aren't smarter or better than you, they've just always believed that you can make money and enjoy yourself at the same time. If you work at a job that pays

well but doesn't fulfill you, you'll spend all your money trying to recapture your happiness when you're not at work.

Note of warning: If you do manage to find a job that pays you to enjoy yourself all day, you will run into some negativity. You will be asked over and over, "When are you going to get a real job?" The naysayers' idea of a real job is a career that makes you miserable. To them, enjoyable jobs can't be real. So, when you get your perfect work game, be prepared for a little Mind Poo from the peanut gallery.

All I ask is that you honestly evaluate what you're doing and see if it is good for you. Just because you've been doing the same thing for ten years doesn't mean you have to do it for another thirty. Maybe you just need to work a little less. It could be that a change in career will satisfy you. If you aren't happy, go from survival to choosing your destiny. If you're having a good time and it doesn't work out, at least you had fun. It sure beats a regular paycheck and a miserable existence. Maybe you need to get that hot dog cart. Working is almost one-third of your entire life, for god's sake. You may as well enjoy it.

What happens when you work too much

Work for the fun of it, and the money will arrive some day.
Ronnie Milsap

Time, Money & Energy

Efficiency is intelligent laziness. David Dunham

You need three factors working for you to get more fun in your life: your available time, your energy level and the amount of extra cash you have in your budget. Let's look at time.

We all have twenty-four hours in a day whether you're the president of the United States or a retired iron-worker living in Costa Rica. It's how you use your time that reflects your quality of life. Is time your pal or your enemy? Are you always trying to beat the clock? Millions of people work extremely hard to have nice things; if you don't have any time to enjoy them, why bother? Should you save a little time for the rainbows, the flowers or your friends?

To begin, you need to figure out where and how you spend your time. The more time you free up from mundane chores, the more time you have to play. Avoid things you dislike. Do you do favors for others with total disregard to your schedule? Do you accept too much responsibility in your life or can you get rid of some of it? Just by deleting fifteen minutes a day, you free up more than one hundred extra play hours in a year.

If you take the time to think it through, there are plenty of ways to become more efficient. Organize your household chores so you can get them done more quickly. Can you do something in thirty minutes instead of forty? Where there is a will there is a way. Do your dishes as you are cooking. Put on a load of laundry before you leave the house in the morning. Think it through.

When you play, play hard; when you work, don't play at all.
Theodore Roosevelt

At work, stop trying to look busy, just get busy and do the things you need to do. Evaluate your use of time and see if you can improve it. Avoid idle chitchat and other time-wasting habits. Batch your tasks and sort out your desk so you're not wasting your valuable moments looking for things. I'm not encouraging you to utilize every second to the maximum in an obsessive way. Just don't waste your time.

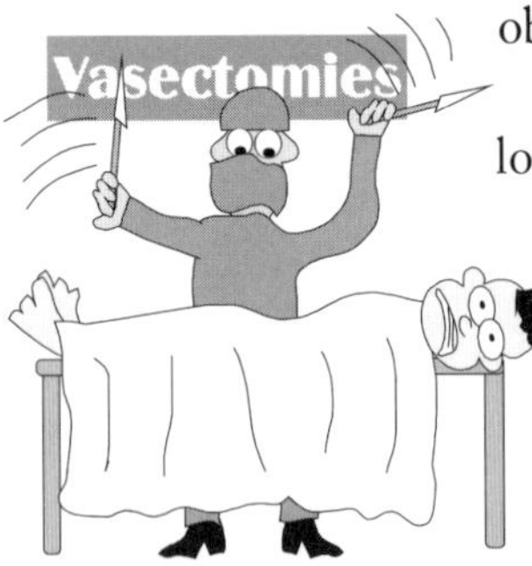

Some things should never be hurried

Maybe you function well at the maximum setting. A lot of people don't. There are some things you don't want to rush. If you're a surgeon, haste may not be the best tactic. Sex should also never be hurried. You don't want to get into a hammock too fast or zip up your fly without checking to see if the coast is clear. Speeding around each and every day will obliterate your peace of mind.

Take life at your pace because if you live at a pace you're not happy with, you'll end up sick with warts growing out of your ears. We all take different roads and travel at different speeds, so go your own way. If you're working smart and effectively, you'll be moving at just the right pace. If things get going too fast, coast for a little while. Take the afternoon off and go down to the park.

As we head out into the burbs for affordable housing, we have added tremendously to our commute times. If you commute one hour each way, you will spend twelve and a half workweeks in one year just on the road. Not to mention the wear and tear on the car, the gas, the maintenance, commuter stress and the increased greenhouse gas emissions. Sure the mortgage is a little cheaper, but is it worth spending twelve and a half workweeks extra to get it?

The ultimate goal of a more effective and efficient life is to provide you with enough time to enjoy some of it. Michael Leboeuf

This formula can apply to anything you do in your life. It takes twenty minutes to blow-dry your hair. Over a year, you would spend 121 hours drying your hair. You don't have to shave your head, just become aware of how you use your time on a day-to-day basis. A few wasted minutes here and there add up to wasted weeks and wasted years. If you choose to sleep nine hours instead of eight each night, in one year that is 15 entire days of sleep. Is this what you really want to be doing with your days?

Simplify your eating habits. Cook meals that take only ten minutes. Simplify your wardrobe so you don't spend all your time choosing. Wear your clothes twice so you do less laundry. Avoid buying clothes that need dry cleaning. It's expensive, time-consuming and uses harmful chemicals. If you spend all your time working, commuting and figuring out the necessities of daily living, no wonder you have no time for fun. Some people think that unless your schedule is filled to the brim, you aren't really living a full life. What a bunch of horse poop.

THE TIME BANDIT

When you begin to assassinate the time bandits, you can open your schedule to fun. If you need some family time or personal time, take it. Devote some time solely to your interests. It will spark creativity, peace and spirituality. Whatever it is you desire, you have to commit some time out of your schedule for it. If you are pressed for time, try short, fun activities instead. Going to the beach may take the whole day, whereas playing a game of catch may take only five minutes. Use your time wisely; once this minute is gone, it's gone. When the clock stops ticking, your time is up.

Defeat the Time Bandit in your life

The man is richest whose pleasures are cheapest. Henry David Thoreau

Once you free up some time you will probably want to have some money as well. There are lots of free forms of entertainment available, but having a few extra dollars around can really expand your horizons. Lack of money can be a huge form of stress. People have enough problems without having financial problems as well. Money can't buy happiness, but it can certainly buy books that can teach you how to be happier.

Are you spending within your means? Do you have credit problems? One bad purchase can screw up your budget entirely. Do not be sucked in by advertising and impulse buying. You may be having fun now, but is your lifestyle sustainable? Any idiot can max out their credit cards. Debt creates obligation. Debt destroys freedom. If you spend more than you have, your punishment will be creditors badgering you, financial stress and guilt. You begin to dread going to the mailbox and avoid answering the phone.

When I returned from my North American bicycle trip I had thirteen different organizations trying to squeeze cash out of me. But sometimes you just have to suck it up and start paying down the debts. Eventually I rid myself of all of them–and that was a very satisfying feeling.

Beware of little expenses. A small leak will sink a great ship
Benjamin Franklin

If you don't have enough money around, you just haven't learned how to use what you have properly. Where does all your money go, anyway? Do you know how much you spend on useless purchases? Let's say you buy a muffin and a latte on your coffee break. For lunch, you have a soup, a sandwich, a beverage and a dessert. Add it all up and you've spent between $15 and $20 in a day. Add that up for a year–are you ready for this one?–and you've spent between $3,750 and $5,000. Once you've wasted a dollar, it's gone forever. Did you really want to give that much money to Starbucks every year? Is there something in your life you're spending gargantuan amounts of money on without even realizing it?

It's a priority thing. Would you rather spend $5,000 on lunches and other crap or would you rather go snorkeling in Fiji for three weeks? Cut out that extra coffee or take your lunch to work. It takes less time to make a lunch than it does waiting to get served and having to wait to pay the bill. Take your lunch and you can make your sandwich exactly the way you want.

Make a game out of using your money wisely. You work hard for what you have, so why give it away for no reason? Either earn more or be smarter with what you have. Use coupons, buy second-hand, watch for sales, travel off-peak, go to garage sales to get a bargain or two. Can you lower your phone bill, cable bill or power bill? Could you carpool to cut down on gas costs? Why sign up for expensive exercise lessons when you can go to the beach or walk around the neighborhood? Are your car or house payments killing you? Maybe you need to downsize. The wiser you are with your cash, the more smiles you'll have. You'll be remembered for who you are, not the value of your car.

Get out of debt as soon as possible. If you have no debts, you are richer than people who do. Pay cash for everything you can. Avoid credit cards because your purchases can haunt you for years. Credit card companies want you to rack up a huge balance so you can pay them 18 percent interest until you wise up.

Are you buying what you need or what the advertisers think you want? Why have a $50,000 car when you just need to get from point A to point B. Is your car a symbol of how cool you are or is it a functional tool? If you bought a $10,000 car, what fun activities could you spend the extra $40,000 on? Buying the best doesn't make you the best.

When you buy an airplane ticket, you can pay $300 in coach or $1,500 in first class. It takes exactly the same amount of time to fly there; you just get an extra snack or two. Fun people realize that you can't buy all the joys out there, but if you budget carefully, you can get a lot more bangs out of your bucks.

Don't stay in bed, unless you can make money in bed.
George Burns

So your budget is cut to the bone and there's still no money for fun? Could you pick up some extra work that would help? Is there something you could sell that you're no longer using? Take that extra money and start a savings account. Save a little here and a little there and when life throws you that inevitable curveball, you'll be ready with a big fat bank account. Get a handle on your money. It's worth the effort.

As you go through this book and learn all the fun habits I've included, you'll come to discover that when you have a fun state of mind you need very little if any money to entertain yourself. Yes, there are lots of fun things to do that cost a good whack of cash. But when you don't have the cash, you make do and enjoy whatever you're doing. There are plenty of low-cost activities you can partake in. Walking in nature, playing Frisbee or watching a sunset are a few. Playing with your children or your lover in the park is a beautiful way to spend an evening. You don't always have to spend money to enjoy yourself.

All good things are wild and free. Henry David Thoreau

Some people have plenty of money and just can't bring themselves to spend a single cent of it. I can't understand why people save their money until they die. Why give the money to your loved ones when you can't even see them enjoy it?

TOMMY THE TIGHTWAD

You deserve to enjoy the fruits of your labor. If you're sitting on a big wad, go out and spend some. Get some toys, do some traveling. Live your life now. Spend some of your money on silly things that make you giggle. It's good to save your money, but once in a while you need to spend it on whatever your heart desires. Go buy some flowers for yourself, get a massage, take a vacation, get out and see the world while you are young and mobile.

I am not suggesting that you spend your money foolishly. But why not lavish it on yourself in the cause of something that you truly desire but thought you didn't really deserve? Don't worry about what other people spend their money on; it's their life. You are only concerned about your life and how much joy and pleasure you can budget into it.

Perhaps I don't have as much money as I would like, but who does? Even the people who have a lot of money are striving to have more. Many of us spend our money on a priority system, with fun being at the back of the pack. Fun people move fun up their list a notch or two so that they always have some form of consistent fun throughout their life. Not only is fun important to me, but the frequency of fun is important.

Let's say I have a fun budget of $2,000. I could go to Hawaii for a week, stay in a nice hotel, eat fancy meals and rent a car, or I could go there for three weeks, live in a hostel, cook my own meals and take the bus around. Or instead of the nice hotel for a week, I could take three separate one-week vacations to three different cities and stay with a friend. I could buy a really expensive set of golf clubs or I could buy a used kayak, a used mountain bike, some camping gear and a used set of golf clubs.

Getting maximum fun out of your money should be a very high priority. Buying lattes is not very important to me, but skiing vacations are. Where are your priorities? Do you need to make more money, go play more, or do you need to go home and be with your family or loved ones? Being clear on your goals and your priorities will help you. If you have a huge desire that you must fulfill, you will get the money for it.

The tooth fairy teaches children that they can sell body parts for money. David Richerby

Even if you make the time and have lots of cash, you are useless without the energy to enjoy your fun activities. How can you have a good time when you're tired? Pace yourself so that you have energy for all areas of your life. You don't want your job or your home life to suck up all your energy. If your brain is in overdrive, you need to collect your thoughts and get recharged. The more you can gain control of your energy levels, the more stamina and fun you will have.

Good energy comes from good healthy habits. Try to isolate the things that take away your energy and practice the ones that give you more. Most of this information is in the health and healing section. You know the drill: avoid coffee and white sugar and make sure you get plenty of sleep.

Being consumed by Mind Poo is one energy robber most of us overlook. Mind Poo takes a lot of mental focus and can destroy whatever happiness you have. Yes, anger can give you bursts of energy to lash out with, but after it's all said and done, I bet you dollars to doughnuts you're exhausted. Worrying takes tons of energy. Playing the "O poor me" song will take away from your life force. In a nutshell, take care of your body, get some exercise and stop tuning into unnecessary Mind Poo.

Once you get your schedule a little more organized, you'll probably find yourself with more energy reserves. Slowing down the pace a little will help you avoid burnout. Getting rid of those unnecessary chores will definitely leave you a little more jubilation juice. Recharge your energy when it's low and make sure you have some left over so you can have some fun after you've done all of life's little chores. Your time, money and energy are extremely precious resources; use them wisely.

Happiness is not a destination it is a method of life. Burton Hills

Giving

Life is more fun when you can share it. Oprah Winfrey

You get out of life what you give. If you plant cactuses, you certainly won't harvest mangoes. Giving is so simple. It can range from money, time, a simple thanks, a heart-felt compliment or just the gift of a smile. Giving is like sex; you probably already know what it is, but if you haven't done it in a long time it's difficult to recall exactly how good it feels. You can receive the most happiness by giving it away to others. You will find that the more you try to give it away, the more it will come back to you.

Great religions tell us that we should give away a percentage of our money to the poor. Give because it feels good, not because you perceive it to be a free ticket to heaven. Some people think that if you give, you're a good person. But if you give with unmentioned expectations, you are not really giving. You are giving gifts with an unwritten agreement that says, "You Owe Me." When you give with the expectation of getting something back, you are really just lending your gifts to others.

I learned the lesson of unconditional giving when I cycled around North America a few years back to promote cycling and environmental awareness. I left with no money and returned 8,100 miles later with a whole new understanding of what unconditional giving really means. I was given meals, a place to sleep, showers, bicycle repairs, clothes, advice, compliments and motivation. These people had no idea who I was or if they would ever see me again, but that didn't matter.

When you are on the receiving end of unconditional giving, you truly understand what a difference a generous person can make to your day. And it wasn't just the rich people. Some of the poorest people I met on that trip were the most generous. The topper was a blind single mother in Portland who gave me enough money to buy a camera so that people who could see would be able to share the visuals from that epic bike ride. It changed my life; I now find it very easy to help strangers financially, emotionally or spiritually. Actually, I find it necessary to do it every once in a while. Something magical happens when you become generous without expectation.

Tragedy will tend to trigger this wave of unconditional giving and support. No matter what the disaster is, no matter what corner of the world it takes place in, people come out of the woodwork to help each other. Whether it's filling sandbags during a flood, giving blood, donating furniture and clothes to a house-fire victim or whatever, it always seems to happen. After you have had a personal experience with people unconditionally giving to you, you will be changed forever.

But why wait for a tragedy? Start the giving and good feelings today. When you find someone who genuinely could use some help and you can fill that gap, you will discover a miracle. "Random acts of kindness and senseless acts of beauty" was a fad for a while and there was good reason for it. It really does put smiles on people's faces.

Giving is easy when it comes from your heart. It will clothe you in a warm, fuzzy, emotional sweater. When you are generous to others, you are good to yourself. How much does it cost you to help someone–five dollars? Maybe ten dollars? Maybe they just need a few minutes of your time. Do starving children upset you? What about the homeless? What have you done to help? Giving will get you closer to God no matter what your religious beliefs are.

Remember to give a warm hug to the one next to you, because that is the only treasure you can give with your heart and it doesn't cost a cent.
George Carlin

There are thousands of charities and community organizations that could use your help. It could be your time, your money or your professional skills. Or maybe they just need someone to sit in the corner and smile at people. Never mind charities; there isn't a single person on this planet who would not benefit from your generosity and kindness. At least you have a huge target market to please. Never pass up the opportunity to do good things for good people and even not so good people.

If you can't afford to give money, try a shove to get a car unstuck, mow a lawn, put a coin in an expired parking meter, bake cookies for people, wash their car. How about giving a meaningful compliment when someone deserves it? There is only one kind of compliment that I recommend sharing and that's a good one. You may make somebody's entire day.

Everyone is good at giving something. The problem is most people just give criticism or share copious amounts of Mind Poo with whoever will listen to them. Criticism is just a way of saying, "Why can't you be more like me or do the things that please me?" They use their self-serving opinions to try to guide you toward the "right" way to live. When you criticize, you are forcing your perception of the world on other people because you want them to understand what poor taste and judgment they have and how much better your judgment is. You come across as a righteous, pompous butthead. What do you expect them to do? Abandon their lives and adopt yours? People like things for their own reasons, and if you can't say anything nice don't say anything at all.

If you ever are asked to give an opinion, candy-coat it in the gentlest way. If their car is a beater, say it's a great beater. If the music is too weird for you, say it has an interesting groove. If their family is psychotic, tell them their family is incredibly unique. If they push you further, give a negative opinion only if they really squeeze it out of you.

Look at a small child drawing a piece of art, then showing it to their parents. Can you imagine how devastating negative criticism would be to that child? Shouldn't all human beings be treated with the enthusiasm and support that small children are usually given? If you want to knock people down a notch, criticize their taste in music, art, cars, houses, their family or their lovers. If you want to live as a more generous spirit, never ever give criticism or advice unless you're specifically asked for it.

Don't abuse your friends and expect them to consider it criticism.
Edgar W. Howe

So, if you should avoid criticism and you don't want to give money, take the easy way and just pass out a smile or two. A smile is just a curve in your face that can set a lot of things straight. Smiling is a cheap way of improving your looks. If you see someone without one, give them one of yours. A smile isn't worth anything until it's given away. Other gifts that cost nothing: emotional support, enthusiasm, compassion, listening. There is no reason why you can't be kind to people. Give friendly feelings to everybody you come in contact with. Be nice to people all the time, not just at Christmas or after a huge tragedy. Be compassionate and understanding wherever you go. Give your gift of goody goodness every chance you can.

Think of all the predicaments you encounter each day that could benefit from you bringing the gift of happiness to the situation. I don't care what kind of career you have, there is always room to give happiness to others throughout your day. Give when you can afford it. Give because you want to, because somebody deserves it. Give because they don't deserve it and you may just touch their heart. You do not have to announce to the world why you are doing it; do it because it needs to be done. Good people who do good actions do not need to cry them out loud.

Be a positive influence on all the lives you touch. Be sensitive and understanding to the people in your world. Everywhere you go, take a gift to people, whether it's a smile or a compliment. By encouraging others around you to laugh and enjoy life, you are giving the gift of pleasure. It's fun when you have a positive impact on someone's life. When you give, you make other people happy and that can only make your day a little brighter.

If you're on the receiving end of gifts, there are two vitally important things you need to do. Accept the gift unconditionally. Whoever gave you the gift probably spent considerable time and effort thinking, choosing or building your gift; it is an extension of their heart. Accept it like it's the best gift in the world–no matter how revolting you may think it is. If it's ugly, give it away at your next garage sale (as long as you know the giver won't be there) or pass it on to someone who really wants it. If you're confronted about where it is, tell them you gave it to someone who loved it even more than you did. If you refuse their offer, you are not only refusing the gift, you are personally disrespecting the giver.

The next part is easy. Say thank you. It is amazing how many people do nice things for others who can't even muster up the energy to spit out two words. Were you over at somebody's for dinner? Phone them the next day and thank them. Did someone give you a gift? Take the time to make a thank-you card and pop it in the mail for them. People just want to be appreciated. Let them know when you do.

Give the world a gift by becoming a fun, happy person. It's all you have to do to leave a successful legacy. Share your happiness and share your fun spirit. If you could give your family or friends one gift, what would it be? A new car, a new house or some kind of gift that will make them happy? If you are happy and having fun, what do you think your partner, kids, friends or peers will receive from you?

Happiness is a by-product of an effort to make someone else happy.
Gretta Book Palmer

A New Beginning

Whether you think you can, or you can't, you are usually right. Henry Ford

What you do on a day-to-day basis reflects who you are. Learning to have fun is like training for a triathlon–slowly, steadily, day by day, you move towards your goal. Many people overtrain and injure themselves. If you hurt yourself in the process of learning to be a fun person, you are going backwards. Yes, try things and fall on your face. Just don't start your program with a hundred-foot cliff dive. Nurture that little fun spirit within you that everybody has.

A PICTURE OF YOU

Be honest with yourself–I mean really honest. Are you happy or are you just putting up with things so that you don't cause any waves? If you try to fool yourself into thinking you're truly happy when you aren't, it makes you the fool. Be honest with all the people around you and the people you do business with. Lying and cheating will repel a fun-filled life. Sometimes we're afraid to tell the truth for fear we will alienate people, that they won't like us anymore. But you have to live with you. If you need to speak the truth, speak it. If telling the truth will cause massive problems, then maybe it is best left unsaid. Honesty is the best policy; just make sure you think through the repercussions of opening your mouth before you actually do.

Look for opportunities to put fun into your life and then do them. Pursue the things that interest you. You will become discouraged, you will run into tragedy, you will get dumped and you will be downcast, but, congratulations, you're still alive. Just keep going; you are the benefactor.

When I'm on my deathbed, I won't be saying, "I wish I had done this" or "I wish I had done that." What about you? When you are cruising around in the afterlife, will your prominent thought be, "Gosh, I'm glad I spent so much time at work?" What will they say at your funeral? "He was a tightwad who always had a scowl on his face, but, man, did he have a nice car." What do you want your legacy to be? When you choose fun, you have made a new beginning.

I believe with all my heart that whoever put us on this planet really would rather see us smile and giggle than shoot each other's brains out. When you choose fun, your whole being begins to sparkle. You laugh more, your health improves and your social circles expand. New places, new faces and new love will weave their way into your life.

Everything in the universe that is beautiful takes time to form, whether it is diamonds, oak trees or mountains. You have the knowledge and the tools to get yourself out of your rut, but you will drift back. Be gentle with yourself. It may take some time to de-serious your personality.

I have heartfelt trust in the fact that no matter who you are or how intelligent you may be, whatever your background or your present situation is, you are capable of having loads of fun in your life. The secret is that everyone has the capacity, tools and technology to make that a reality. It's time to play.

Peter Pigbum was ready to fill his fun bag to the very top

Carry a legacy of delight wherever you go and with whomever you deal with. Let your heart feel good, smile whenever you can and sleep well at night. It's your life. You should enjoy it as much as humanly possible. It doesn't matter how much fun you have now because you can always have more. It is impossible to overdose on smiles or laughter. Joy is infinite.

Move past the monsters of fear, anger and sadness. Clarify what you want out of life. Imagine being silly once or twice a day. See yourself surrounded by quality fun players. Go out and make new friends, see exciting places, travel to new levels of adventure, break through old stupid walls that hold you back. Whoever has the most laughs wins.

All these elements are reciprocal. The more life experiences you have, the more fun you will have. The more fun you have, the more you will experience life in all its multi-dimensional beauty. The universe is unfolding as planned. Instead of paddling upstream all the time, just go with the flow of the river. If you continue to fight it, you will eventually become so exhausted that you will end up floating downstream anyway.

Your fun knowledge can only grow from here on in. You're on this planet to learn, expand, interact and share your gifts, skills and talents. Wish to bring happiness to your fellow travelers as you journey through this crazy world of ours. Avoid finding fault with any person–no matter how much they make your blood boil.

Be a person whose name carries a smile wherever it goes. Avoid fun procrastination in all its forms and never under any circumstances plan to be happy tomorrow when you could be happy today. Believe that there are thousands of people secretly planning to make you laugh or help you experience happiness. Expect to laugh, giggle and enjoy your way through every single day. Get a good grip on what life has to offer and never let anybody ruin your fun. Fun isn't a secret, it's a choice. You will gain momentum and begin to layer your mini-happiness victories on top of each other and, before you know it, you will be wallowing in fun and good times.

Your beliefs create your world, so if you believe that you deserve a fun life, you will have it. Fun is a state of mind that does not depend on other activities, people, or places. Excercise it daily and you can have that feeling anytime you desire. At the end you can look back and say, "Wow, I achieved so much, had so many good times, good friends and wonderful experiences. I feel as if I've somehow positively influenced and touched so many lives. But best of all, I had loads of fun."

I have only two kinds of days: happy and hysterically happy.
Allen J. Lefferdink

Goal Setting

Bite off more than you can chew, then chew like crazy. Anonymous

1. Get out a pen and a piece of paper and ask yourself this, "If I knew I could not fail, what fun activities would I like to participate in?" Cost, experience and availability are irrelevant at this point. Let your mind wander. No matter how crazy your thought is just write it down. Scuba diving in the Bahamas? Mountain climbing in the Rockies? (If you are having a mental block go to the website www.discoverfun.com–you will find an extensive list of fun things to do.) When you begin, write them down as fast as you can–no restrictions. Take three minutes and write as many as you can. Are you ready? GO...

2. Then look at your list and decide what three goals would give you the most pleasure. What have you always wanted to do but just were either too busy, or didn't think it was possible? When you have circled your top five goals take out a new piece of paper. Of these, which goal would have the most potent impact on your level of fun and pleasure? Write that goal at the top of the list. Then write down the second most important goal, and so on.

3. Then take your number one goal and make a plan for you to achieve this goal in the next year. Write down all the things that you could do to make it a reality. What actions would you need to take? The more detailed steps you can describe and write down, the easier it will be for you to make your goal a reality. All you have left to do now is add in some enthusiasm and some action. You will accomplish a lot in a very short time with clearly written goals.

You are the only individual on the planet who can spell out in detail what will make you a happy soul. You may doubt if this whole goal-setting situation works. But what if it does? What if you have the time of your life?

Plan more than you can do, then do it. Anonymous

We have a list of more than 500 different fun activities on our website. If you are ever thinking that you are bored, this list will solve your problem.

What people are typing....

I can't believe how many different ideas for fun you have. This fun list is the Thesaurus of Fun!
Tracey Jacobsen

A must have resource for anybody who enjoys life.
Katie Wooley

The 500 fun list has shown me how regular my normal fun is and how much more fun my fun can be.
John Timpson

Categories

Adventure
Bored
Creative
For Dangerous Minds
Expensive Things
Family Fun
Fitness
Food and Drink
Free Games to Play
Friends
Home Entertainment
Inside
Kid Fun
Love and Dating Games
Naughty by Nature
Party Themes
Places to Go
Photography
Public
Somethings Gotta Give
Spontanaeous
Strange
Stress Management
Special Days
Sports
Summer
Travel
Web Games
Winter
Fun at Work

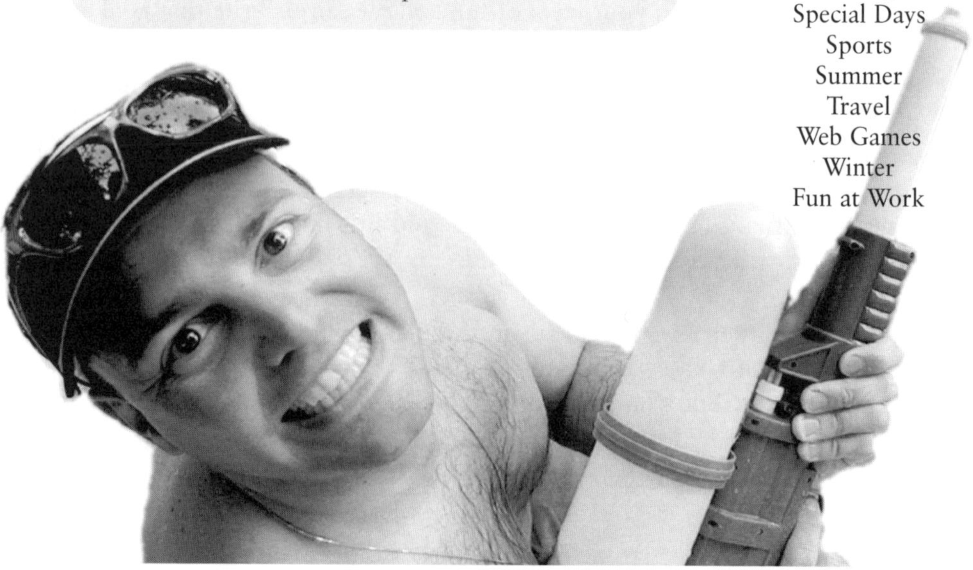

Feedback

You do have the magic to make people have fun. Fran Bryant

I love this website! Jeff Stickelmeyer

Fantastic website! Wesley Miller

Come discover our award-winning website www.discoverfun.com. We have been featured on CNN Radio, the Wall Street Journal Radio Network and MTV. It has a plethora of informationon on all the dimensions of fun.

- Download desktop backgrounds for your computer
- Win Prizes!
- Get color versions of the cartoons
- Discover information on crazy fun rituals
- Check out our April Foool's Pranks Section
- Check out our photo and video galleries
- Check out articles on fun people, careers and activities
- Download media clips
- See the 500 List of Fun Things to Do

When a coconut and a head collide, there is a hollow sound; is it from the coconut?

The Fun Report

Find out why thousands of people are signing up for **The Fun Report.**

95% of subscribers stay subscribers
You receive special fun inspiration
Automatically signed up for contests
Funnest newsletter on the web
Alerts you to new content on the site
Keeps you in the loop

Your "Fun Report" is killer. Richard Bender

Thanks for the continuing laughs. Getting your "Fun Report" is a high point in my work day.
Suzee Knight

I sit alone and laugh till I cry almost at your video clips from your "Fun Report" - I highly recommend it.
Jan Dean

Go sign up now at **www.discoverfun.com**

Privacy Policy

We will not under any circumstances give or sell this information to any mailing list or telemarketing company anywhere in the known or unknown universe.

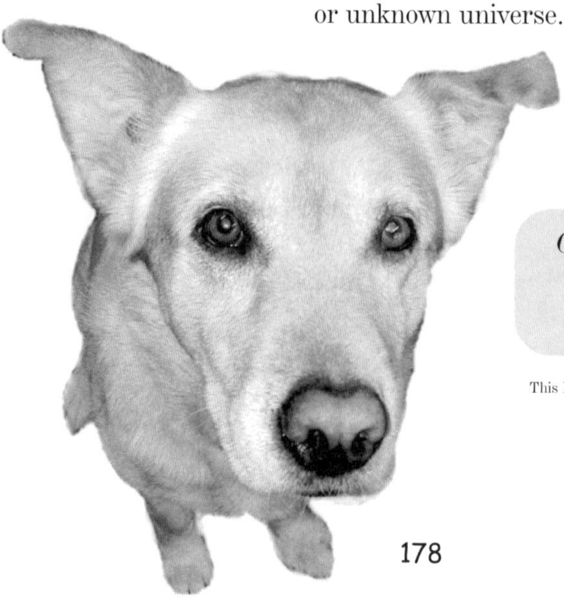

On the Internet, nobody knows you're a dog.
Peter Steiner

This Email newsletter was not tested on animals

Ted Schredd is a best-selling author and inspirational keynote speaker, seminar leader and expert in adding more fun to your daily experience. Ted motivates and inspires people to enjoy this little adventure we call life. He helps people move past the restrictions that hold them back and re-instills the belief that we all deserve to have more fun than we ever thought possible. Ted provides practical tools and great advice on how to escape the shackles of Mind Poo and to transplant groups and individuals into the world of fun.

Ted Schredd on MTV

Call the office 1.888.SUCH.FUN

www.discoverfun.com/speaker/

Judging by the overwhelming number of people that attended your presentation, and from the incredible feedback, it is obvious that the information you shared, in our opinion is priceless.
La Funny Girl Entertainment

Your presentation was "unforgettable." It was a great success and the feedback has been terrific.
Vance Financial Group

Ted Schredd has a unique perspective on life that emphasizes fun and a sense of holistic harmony.
Synergy Adventure Training

The Fun Police

The Fun Police™ is a unique form of entertainment for conventions, special events and large public gatherings. The Fun Police™ combines performance art, interactivity and a whole lot of laughs.

The Fun Police™ deliver such an awesome experience for their carefully chosen prey, they are able to hold considerable influence with their target audience. The Fun Police™ offer a creative and memorable experience to get your event noticed and remembered.

THE FUN POLICE™ ARE POSITIVE

THE FUN POLICE™ ARE INTERACTIVE

THE FUN POLICE™ ARE MEMORABLE

Fun Officers do their absolute best to interact, engage and entertain the event participants. If you would like more information please contact the office.

Call 1-888 SUCH FUN

www.discoverfun.com/funpolice/

The Fun Police;
We will fly anywhere for money

Ted Schredd's first book, a Canadian bestseller, chronicles the tales of his 8,100-mile bicycle ride around North America. A yearning for adventure takes Schredd by bicycle from Vancouver, British Columbia, down the west coast of the United States, across the country to Texas, on towards Florida, up the coast through New York, and then north to Ottawa. Wacky cartoons and humorous, captivating stories reveal his encounters along the way. Experience "Confused Biker Syndrome," the Californian hill from hell, and ketchup-eating raccoons. Meet farmer Bob, Tammi the exotic dancer, and Duke, the Texan whose father raises alligators.

Published by Whitecap Books. 200 pages, $14.95.US

"Schredd's journey makes for a light-hearted, high spirited quick read."
Naomi Gollogy - Willamette Week

"A humorous read that avoids the dreaded, dry, travelogue format."
Andrew McCredie - North Shore News

"This book is the incredible record of his journey, complete with cartoons to bring the wacky days to life" Fittingly Yours Magazine

"I was hooked from the start, entertained, amused, and enlightened by each morsel." Kirsten Fraser - Where Magazine

"A threat to literature."
Fiona McCaw - Monday Magazine, Victoria, BC

"The Cycling Adventures of Coconut Head was laugh out loud funny!"
Dean Payne - Vancouver, BC

Order from
www.discoverfun.com

8,100 mile bike trip

The Fun Store

You loved the F Word and now you want to have more fun

Come to the fun store and check out our cool products:

Confetti Cannons

Our best seller. Using compressed air, these cannons blast confetti up to 60 feet in the air

Freestyle Footbags

Ebooks

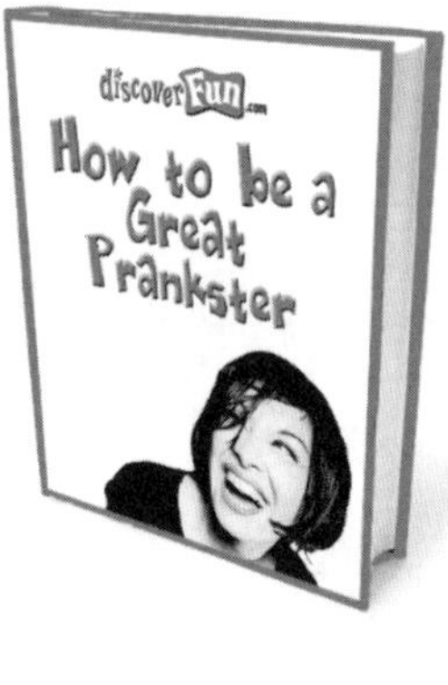

And new, unique fun products are added all the time. Check it out:

www.discoverfun.com/funstore

Arnold
Kentucky
Coyote Kevin
Cheewwka
Craig
Carolyn
Elizabeth
Peter Purple
The Shander
The Gupper
Rockin' Bob
Lukey
Goo
Loo
Portman
Tanis
Al & Edith
Larry Hope
Little Smart
Bender the Brander
Bruce
Scotty
Dr. Feel Good
and everyone else who has taught me something about fun.

I hate quotations. Ralph Waldo Emerson